BENT HALOS AND OTHER SAINTLY STORIES

BENT HALOS
AND OTHER
SAINTLY STORIES

The Lives of One Hundred
Saintly Men and Women

Rev. C.T. Thomas

ALBA·HOUSE   NEW·YORK

SOCIETY OF ST. PAUL, 2187 VICTORY BLVD., STATEN ISLAND, NEW YORK 10314

ST PAULS

Library of Congress Cataloging-in-Publication Data

Thomas, C.T.
  Bent halos and other saintly stories: the lives of one hundred
saintly men and women / [compiled by] C.T. Thomas.
      p.   cm.
  ISBN 0-8189-0862-9
  1. Catholic Biography. 2. Christian saints Biography.
I. Thomas, C.T.
BX4651.2.B44   1999
282'.092'2 — dc21   99-23049
[B]   CIP

Produced and designed in the United States of America by the
Fathers and Brothers of the Society of St. Paul,
2187 Victory Boulevard, Staten Island, New York 10314-6603,
as part of their communications apostolate.

ISBN: 0-8189-0862-9

Printing Information:

Current Printing - first digit   1   2   3   4   5   6   7   8   9   10

Year of Current Printing - first year shown

1999   2000   2001   2002   2003   2004   2005   2006   2007   2008

ACKNOWLEDGMENTS

This work would not have been accomplished without the tireless help of Ândy Andracki who got the whole project going, and without the assistance of Joann Andracki, Mary Dorrian and other St. Timothy friends.

Alban Butler's *Lives of the Saints* provided resources and guidance. (Edited by Herbert Thurston, Kenedy and Sons, New York, 1926)

Another guiding source was *The Catholic Encyclopedia.* (1907 edition, Robert Appleton Company, New York)

The library of the Pontifical College Josephinum in Columbus, Ohio was a treasure chest of information.

Mary Kay Hummel has given permission for the use of her material on St. Isidore published in "Plowshares," the newsletter of the Ohio Catholic Rural Life Conference.

Salesiana Publishers have granted permission for my use of the material on St. John Bosco from their publication *The Biographical Memoirs of St. John Bosco Vol II* edited by Giovanni Battista Lemoyne, New Rochelle, NY: Salesiana, 1966.

TABLE OF CONTENTS

CHAPTER IV

BENT HALOS AND OTHER SAINTLY STORIES

CHAPTER I

FRANCIS DE SALES

The kid shouldn't have poked the monkey anyway

At a previous parish, I fearlessly chaperoned high school ski trips, college retreats and senior citizen tours, but none of these adequately prepared me for supervising five first graders at the city zoo. I thought I had agreed to be one of six adults chaperoning 30 students, but when we got to the zoo, they divided the class into five groups, each led by one adult!

The day was exhausting. They were too small to hit, too smart to threaten, and too fast to catch. By 2:30 P.M. I was reduced to yelling obscenities at one urchin who insisted on poking his hand through the fence around "Monkey Island" to jab awake a lethargic lemur. The animal turned and scratched the boy's hand. The child was more scared than hurt, but just to be safe, we washed the wound in the duck pond and put some sun screen on it.

Later, I figured out the problem. I had forgotten to pray to St. Francis de Sales. In his gentleness and kindness, he would never have screamed at the children, let alone steal from their lunches.

In his guide for Christian living called *Introduction to the Devout Life*, he writes, "The person who possesses Christian meekness is affectionate and tender toward everyone; he is disposed to forgive and excuse the frailties of others; the goodness of his heart appears in a sweet affability that influences all his words and actions."

Was this guy for real?

Even his friend and biographer Jean Camus wasn't sure. So, having more curiosity than good manners, Camus drilled a peephole into de Sales' rooms where he could spy on the already famous writer, confessor, bishop and preacher.

What he found was that Francis was completely true to his own advice. He got up in complete silence so he wouldn't wake up his valet. He prayed, wrote, ate, and prayed again. The same courtly manners and Christ-like gentleness shown to princes and the world in books and sermons were there in private too — for cleaning ladies, cooks and dishwashers, and all who had access to Francis's little domestic world.

Camus didn't need his peephole. He could have questioned thousands of individuals who had been touched by Francis's humble, good heart.

Francis de Sales was born into the nobility of Savoy, received a great education, and was already a Doctor of the Law by age 24. He could easily have been elected to the Senate of Savoy as his father wished him to be. But Francis wanted to be a priest instead. He got his wish, and later became Bishop of Geneva in 1602.

That may not have been a good idea. Catholics in Geneva at that time were so unpopular that the new bishop had to guide his diocese from outside the city. Calvinists were running things there across the beautiful lake from the mountains of Savoy.

Catholics were trying to win back territories that had gone over to Protestantism. But whereas some were attempting to do so by military force or the prosecutions of the Inquisition, de Sales would do it with charm, intelligence, and graciousness.

He went into areas that might have contained just a few Catholics here and there. He preached, wrote little pamphlets that people re-copied by hand, and gently explained Catholic teachings and worship.

Francis was interested in leading his people to holiness. But unlike mystics who saw withdrawal from the world as the path to such a goal, he wanted to pursue sanctity in the world, in the joys and sorrows of everyday life. His guidance was sound for those shut away in monasteries, but it was equally valuable for those who had jobs to go to, and families to raise.

He preached and wrote with a profound depth of understanding of the faith, but also with outstanding clarity and simplicity. The 26 volumes of his collected letters and works are so approachable by so many that he's been honored as the patron of the Catholic press.

Spiritual advisors and preachers down through the years have been guided by his great insight into human nature as well as by his homey maxims. A favorite of the latter reads: "A spoonful of honey attracts more flies than a barrel full of vinegar."

Francis de Sales' feast is celebrated January 24th right before the beginning of Catholic press month.

Caring and compassion in Krakow

Years ago, as a young assistant priest, I returned with the pastor from Saturday supper to find that some kind and generous parishioner had left a large, yellow sheet cake on the back porch for us to enjoy.

Later, I got to thinking that that cake would fit in great with our Saturday evening ritual of a double bourbon and some dessert while we watched a popular new TV show called MASH. But the cake, I felt, needed icing to be a real success.

So I rummaged through the cook's books in the kitchen until I came across a recipe for Seven Minute Chocolate Frosting. An hour and a half, four bowls, and one bent ladle later, the frosting was ready. I had to smear it on quickly because the show was starting.

We settled in to enjoy ourselves, but as he bit into his cake, the pastor wore a funny look on his face. When I tasted mine, I understood why. The yellow sheet cake was actually a big pan of corn bread.

St. John Kanty would never have made the same mistake. He didn't eat cake. He didn't eat pie either. As a matter of fact, he didn't eat lots of things. He wasn't dieting for his health though. It was for penance and for solidarity with the poor. In the long run, maybe it was a healthy thing to do after all, since he lived to be 83.

John was a Polish priest who taught at the university of

Krakow until envious colleagues got him tossed out. He was sent to a country parish where he wasn't very welcome either, at least at first. But his parishioners warmed to his quiet goodness even though his sermons may have gone over their heads.

They were sorry to see him go when he was recalled to the university where he spent most of the rest of his life as a teacher of Sacred Scripture.

He proved to be more than a teacher to his students though. He was a counselor, a confessor, a friend. He sacrificed what little he had to help feed those who were hungry, and begged for donations to help the wider circle of poor in Krakow.

John's one great desire was never realized. He wanted to be martyred by the Turks for preaching Christ. So he journeyed to Jerusalem and spoke on the street corners. The Turks listened, but ignored what he said, and he had to go home unmartyred.

Four pilgrimages on foot from Poland to Rome served to increase his stamina both for work and for sacrifice, and his charity toward all made him loved and respected in his own lifetime and throughout Polish history.

John died in 1473 and was canonized in 1767 by Pope Clement XIII. His feast is December 23rd. Those who get a Latin-English dictionary from Santa might want to know that his motto read:

> Conturbare cave —
> non est placare suave;
> Infamare cave —
> *nam revocare grave.*

If you still have a few friends on your gift list who think they have everything they need already, try passing around some chocolate iced corn breads. They may seem way too sweet at first, but the idea is to balance their taste with a good slug of sour mash.

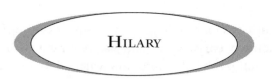

HILARY

> ## As a songwriter, he was wise to keep his day job

When St. Hilary was in exile in the East, he came across St. Ephraim's idea of using hymns to teach sound doctrine and oppose heresy. He took the practice home with him to France, and is said to be the first writer of Latin hymns.

Irving Berlin he wasn't though, and his songs never became that popular. But if your church uses Paluch's Missalette, you might recently have sung a few lines of his "O Radiant Light," a compact ditty that attempts to place Jesus in proper position alongside the Father and the Spirit. This was Hilary's real quest and lifelong struggle. He suffered for it, but never abandoned it.

Hilary came from a noble family in what was called Gaul (modern day France), and was well educated in the philosophy and the pagan culture of Greece and Rome. He found, though, that ancient myths couldn't satisfy his search for deeper meaning in life, and turned to the study of the Hebrew and Christian Scriptures instead.

He quickly came to reject polytheism (the belief in more than one god), and was overwhelmed with the dignity and loftiness of the name given God by God in the book of Exodus, "I Am Who Am," — the one and only, the eternal.

He came to believe in Christ, was baptized, and soon was chosen bishop of Poitiers in 353. We're not sure what his wife and daughter thought of his new job.

Yes, like many bishops of the early Church, Hilary was a family man. By this time in the Church's history, it was unlikely for a person to be consecrated bishop and then be allowed to marry, but it was still possible for already married men to become bishops.

Were they then required to live like celibates? St. Jerome wrote that they all did just that, but how would he know? Besides, there is lots of evidence to the contrary.

As for Hilary, we know he did indeed lead the life of a bachelor for years, because he was forced to travel far from home.

The emperor exiled him to Asia Minor because he refused to go along with the government's toleration of Arianism, a heresy which saw Jesus as not truly divine.

In exile, Hilary kept up his criticism of the Arians and of all the bishops who strayed from sound doctrine, telling the emperor that they were constantly making new creeds, condemning old ones, then condemning their condemnations, then repenting, then starting all over again.

There were lots of Arians in the area Hilary had been exiled to, and he became such a thorn in their side, that it was they who begged the emperor to let the man go home.

Hilary was received in triumph in Poitiers where he continued to fight Arianism in the West just as Athanasius had done in the East. He died around 368, and his feast is celebrated January 14th.

Besides his few unappreciated hymns, and his letters and treatises against Arianism, Hilary also wrote commentaries on Scripture and theology. A very comforting idea for those who wonder about the reason for our existence is offered by St. Hilary: God, who is perfectly happy, created angels, and us, simply to share that happiness.

Get the mortgage papers out of the salsa

Moving to a different parish is always confusing the first year because one does not know all the traditions of the new place. This Christmas, for example, I was surprised to see the grade school faculty all marching toward the rectory when the last day of school was over. I asked the secretary why they were all headed my way, and she said, "Why for the school staff Christmas party of course. Didn't you know about that?"

No! I didn't know about that, and I had nothing ready for them to eat or drink! Then, I remembered something I had noticed earlier in the day and breathed a sigh of relief. I fired up the parish van and had the doors all open for them to pile in as I told them we were going for a short ride to our party.

The local bank has one of those beautiful old lobbies, all marble and bronze. For the holiday customers, it had set out a huge table of goodies: cookies, pastries, nut breads, boxes of chocolates, steaming pots of coffee and tea, and a glistening crystal punch bowl filled with a delicious frosty drink.

We had a wonderful time. We could do the gift exchange right there, and luckily someone had received a fifth of rum that enlivened the punch considerably. All day long, busy bank customers had ignored the treats as they hurried out the door to spend more money. So there was a great deal for us to enjoy. Occasionally, I had to talk one of the teachers into depositing or withdrawing something at the teller windows to allay suspicions. No one interfered with us for the longest time, except to ask us to go more softly on the carols, especially the Hark the Herald Angels one.

Finally, a snooty assistant manager started slyly drifting our way. I tried slipping behind a pillar, but I could tell he thought he was on to something as he kept me in sight. It took some effort, but I managed to save our party. I pleaded with the football coach until he agreed to refinance his house. We were home free.

I imagine Margaret Bourgeoys must have felt the same way when she set foot in New France, at Montreal in 1653. All her life she had wanted to be a teacher of children, and her dream was about to come true. It hadn't always looked that way.

Her mother died when she was young, and she had to take charge of the house. Later, both the Carmelites and the Poor Clares turned down her applications. A local Order of Sisters she joined in France fell apart when people refused to support the novel idea of uncloistered Sisters.

When Governor de Maisonneuve came home from Canada to look for a schoolmistress for his new colony, Margaret's prospects brightened considerably. She met Maisonneuve through the governor's sister and volunteered for the job right away.

During her first five years at Montreal, Margaret visited the sick, helped raise children, nursed soldiers and sailors, and finally opened a school in 1658. She sensed the work would be too much for her alone. So she went back to France twice to recruit more Sisters to join her.

In 1676, Margaret's group of 48 became the Congregation of Notre Dame, the first religious order founded in the New World. Margaret founded more schools for both French and Indian children, and her order would eventually have over two hundred members.

But her work was always hard. She gave away her bed during her first winter here, she lost a beloved niece in a fire that destroyed her first convent, and Church authorities continued to resist her idea of Sisters working out among the people instead of in cloistered communities.

Even at the age of 80, she was still sacrificing herself for God and others. A young Sister suddenly became sick. Margaret prayed, "O my God, why will Thou not accept the sacrifice of my life, rather than deprive the Community of that dear and excellent child." The young Sister recovered. Margaret died on January 8, 1700.

Margaret was always appreciative of those who gave themselves to teaching. Unlike many religious Orders, she even accepted penniless women without dowries into her group. I think she would have approved of our appreciation party at the bank except maybe for the last part. When the lobby started to close at 4:00, the six of us who were still reveling had to grab what we could carry and crowd into the drive-through booth which was open till 6:00.

Sava the Enlightener

Maybe he can help turn the corner once again

Americans of many faiths had their attention focused on the safety and success of the U.N. and U.S. forces in Bosnia-Herzegovina during the '90's. Some among us may have even added an extra appeal for the intercession of Sava the Enlightener, patron saint of Serbia and its first homegrown archbishop.

The Serbs are part of a greater mass of Slavic people who migrated long ago from their original homeland into places like Russia and Poland, and south into what used to be called Yugoslavia. The southern Slavs were brought to Christianity by Saints Cyril and Methodius around the year 863.

Eventually, some became more closely attached to Western or Roman Christianity, the Croats for example. Others followed religious traditions centered in the Orthodox East. The Serbs are among the latter.

Around 1160, Stephen Nemanya was seeking to build up a united Serbia, independent, and free from domination by the Byzantine Empire centered in Constantinople. He looked to three strong sons to help him, but the youngest was a disappointment. He ran away to a monastery.

Rastko Nemanya wanted to be a hermit on one of those "inaccessible" cliff retreats surrounding Mount Athos. Instead, he was given the job of delivering bread from the main monastery to the hermits who did live on the "inaccessible" cliff retreats surrounding Mount Athos.

From being a disappointment to his father, he moved to be an inspiration. Stephen resigned from politics and joined Rastko, now the monk Sava, at a monastery called Khilandari, where the retired ruler died.

Sava could have stayed on in any monastery of his choosing since he was too old to keep his bread route and he became abbot on Mount Athos. But there was trouble at home.

Stephen had divided responsibility for Serbia between Sava's brothers, Stephen II and Vulkan. Violence and intrigue resulted, but the brothers retained enough good sense to appeal to Sava to come back to make peace between them.

Sava brought more than political peace though. He ushered in an era of spiritual revival. He founded monasteries where the monks were organized to work as preachers and pastors directly among the people. He encouraged native Serbian vocations, and eventually won approval from Constantinople for the formation of a native Serbian archdiocese.

Sava wanted to build bridges to Catholic Rome as well. He successfully petitioned the pope to recognize his brother Stephen as the first king of Serbia, and attended his crowning in 1221.

Towards the end of his life, Archbishop Sava made two journeys to Jerusalem, and even realized his dream of visiting Mt. Sinai. On his return home though, he grew increasingly exhausted, and died on Sunday, January 14th, past the age of seventy.

Sava's feats approach mythological proportions among Serbian peasants. It is said that before his time farmers would plow a row of soil and then drag the plow back across the field in reverse to do another. The Enlightener taught them to turn the corner instead and plow back the other way. Another legend has it that cottages used to be lit and cooled by opening doors until Sava taught folks about windows.

On a more spiritual level, Sava is remembered for his humility (he once called himself just a lazy monk); his gentleness and leniency as an abbot dealing with young monks; and his gifts as a reconciler.

Even if his advice on plowing and air conditioning isn't much needed anymore, surely his other insights might help all peacemakers in the Balkans today.

FRUCTUOSUS

Looking for help in all the wrong places

The kids who go to our grade school here are just too good. The other day I went over to see the dean of discipline to find out who owed detention hours from before Christmas break. Of course, the hours always double if they have not been served in a timely fashion. The drain gutters on the rectory roof needed to be cleaned out, and I was sure I could get loads of free help from kids serving extra detention.

So I asked him how many children he had in detention and how many hours they could "give" me. "Sorry, Father," he said, "Can't help you. The kids have been really good so far this year." Obviously, I couldn't believe that. So I went through a litany of things I always remembered as fun.

"You mean to tell me no one has gotten into teachers' cars to turn the lights on, then locked the doors and run to the office to piously report a problem in the parking lot?" "No," he said. "Well what about the cafeteria? Has anyone been putting rubber bands on the kitchen sink sprayers so the cooks get a shot of water in the face as soon as they turn the tap on?" "Why of course not!" he shot back.

"No locking all the bathroom stalls and squirming out on their belly so that no one can get in?"

"Sorry, Father, I can't say we've had any of that either."

"Well surely, someone's misbehaved along the way."

"Now that you mention it. We did have some second-graders caught throwing mud balls at the dumpster."

"Do you think they'd be any good on ladders?" But, by then, he wasn't listening to me anymore. He just kind of sat there staring out into space.

I felt like the governor who questioned St. Fructuosus and his two deacons. Try as he might, he could find no real evil in them, but he needed a conviction nonetheless. The Emperor Valerian had issued orders that Christian priests and bishops must offer sacrifice to the pagan gods.

Fructuosus, as bishop of the important city of Tarragona in Spain, was an obvious target of such an official persecution. He was arrested on January 16th, 259 and brought before Aemilianus the following week.

The governor asked the bishop if he were aware of the emperor's orders, and the bishop said no. Aemilianus told Fructuosus that he was ordered to worship the gods. The bishop replied that he worshiped the one God who "has made heaven and earth, the sea, and all that is in them."

Aemilianus insisted that if the gods were not worshiped then the images of the emperor would not be adored. But, getting nowhere with Fructuosus, he turned to the first deacon instead.

"Do not listen to the words of Fructuosus," he warned him.

"I worship God almighty," the deacon replied.

The governor may have been exasperated at this point, or at least confused, because he asked the second deacon, "Do you not also worship Fructuosus?" That deacon said, "No, I do not worship Fructuosus, but I worship the One whom he worships."

In the end, the governor sentenced all three to he burned at the stake. The Acts of the Martyrs has the execution being carried out on January 21st.

Fructuosus shares a feast day with the famous St. Agnes. Much more is believed about her than about the bishop, even though less is actually known concerning her.

Stuck on the chair of Peter

We knew our mother was getting older when she started insisting on a base runner whenever she came to bat. All the family playing that year voted, and she won: 32 to 28. It's not that those of us in the minority wanted to begrudge an eighty year-old woman the courtesy of a base runner. It was the precedent we were worried about.

What if uncle Fred with his cataracts at short stop wanted a change in the infield fly rule? Could a person slide into third feet-first if it was guarded by cousin Sallie who was six months pregnant? Where would the exceptions end? When would our pastime quit being baseball and end up being just another backyard game?

Knowing where to draw the line was a lifelong concern of Peter Canisius. This son of a wealthy Dutch family disappointed his father by refusing to marry a wealthy young woman and becoming a priest instead.

While he was a student at Cologne, Peter became aware of the major challenge facing the Church of his age: the need for reform. Lutherans and other Protestants would pursue that reform outside Roman Catholicism. Peter chose a different track.

He would work within the Church to change things that needed changing; he would meet the Protestants half-way on measures they could both agree on; but he would doggedly uphold principles of Catholic doctrine and Church authority, especially papal authority. He told a friend, "Whoever adheres to the Chair of Peter is my man. With Ambrose, I desire to follow the Church of Rome in every respect."

As Peter grew in intellect and stature, it became clear that Rome had a champion as formidable as he was loyal. After attending a retreat given by one of Ignatius Loyola's first Jesuits, he decided to become one too: number eight to be exact.

He taught at three German universities, and founded five colleges in Germany and Austria. He was an advisor to an emperor, to several popes in a row, and to the great reforming Council of Trent. He was a Jesuit provincial in several places and a much sought after speaker throughout central Europe.

It was Peter's conviction that Protestants could be won back to Rome not by wars of religion and bouts of persecution, but by persuasion, debate, and good example. He is credited with helping to return major parts of the German-speaking world to Catholicism by tireless preaching, teaching and counseling.

In Bavaria, Bohemia and Austria, Canisius worked with sympathetic rulers and leaders to bring about reform and peaceful dialogue. In this, he was following a maxim of Ignatius himself, who told his men to work with influential persons in important places so that, once these folk met with spiritual improvement, they might "cause the profit to spread to others that obey their authority or follow their directions."

Peter Canisius' influence continued long after his death on December 21st, 1597. He wrote what became called a Triple Catechism — hundreds of questions and answers about the Faith written on three levels: one for children, one for teens and one for college students. The catechism went through 400 editions in the course of 150 years. It was so widely used in Germany that to "open a Canisius" meant to consult a catechism.

PAULA

From riches to rags, from palaces to penances

At a parish council meeting years ago, I remember being asked if I liked my assignment and if I had many years left to serve as pastor. I replied that I did indeed enjoy my work there and that I planned to stay for as long as the money held out.

At that, a finance committee member commented that the money would hold out longer if I wouldn't buy things like 150 family size, holiday ice cream cake rolls. This gave me a chance to expound on the wisdom of buying in bulk and at post-holiday prices, getting a large $8.99 roll for only $6.50.

Another member agreed with me regarding my sharp business sense but added that the rolls seemed to be melting in the back of my '88 Buick Roadmaster station wagon. I immediately took the opportunity to remind the council of my previous recommendation that the parish invest $8,500 in a new walk-in freezer, pointing out that, had we made that move when I asked, the ice cream rolls wouldn't be getting soft in the winter sun in the back of my car.

Someone started to suggest I park my car in the garage until she was reminded that that's where I had put the 30 foot Halloween float I had made with its 26 colored statues of "Saints of Early America." The meeting went downhill from there.

St. Jerome had similar problems in dealing with people who did not appreciate his genius. He was roundly disliked by many in Rome who simply didn't understand him. St. Paula though was a notable exception.

She was a widow of great lineage and wealth, a true blue blood of the old Roman aristocracy. But her money and position couldn't save her from heartache when her husband died at a young age. Paula went on to suffer more grief and loss at the deaths of several of her children.

But her personal tragedy never led her to bitterness. It led her to God instead. Her friend St. Marcella introduced her to Christianity, and St. Jerome helped her to a deeper understanding of Scripture. Paula's wealth was soon finding its way to needy people of all kinds, and her active social life gave way to one of quiet reflection and prayer, mixed with visits to the sick and suffering.

Eventually, Paula and her surviving daughter Eustochium journeyed east to catch up with St. Jerome who finally settled in Jerusalem. When she wanted to tour the Holy Land, Roman officials kept offering her hospitality in palaces and royal courts, but she chose simpler places instead.

Paula came to adopt the very strict regimen of monastic life in the East — long hours of prayer, fasting, and reflection. But she combined these ascetic practices with her study of Hebrew and the books of the Bible that Jerome was translating. She used the last of her wealth to found a hospital for pilgrims to Jerusalem and monasteries for both men and women.

Jerome came to rely on her as a true helpmate and one of the few people in his life who were truly dear to him on a personal level. By the time Paula died on January 26th, 404, she and Jerome had worked together for 20 years. His eulogy for her in his letter 108 is said by some to be his very best. Jerome seems to have thought so too. Towards its end he writes: "As you see, I have built you a monument more enduring than bronze, which no passage of time will be able to destroy."

> **Sell the daughter before she empties the larder**

Brigid's father threw her in his chariot and tore off down the road to see the king. His intention? To sell her.

Dubthach had tried to be patient, but her charity toward the poor had finally exasperated him. First, it was the milk she'd given away; then the family's butter; finally, his very own best clothes. She'd make a decent slave. Her mother had been one too.

He told her to wait in the chariot while he went in to see the clan's king in Leinster. Of course he couldn't wear his sword in to visit the sovereign. So he left it outside with his daughter.

Big mistake. By the time he got back with the king, she had given that away too, to a leper no less. Forget about haggling, he would just give her away. But the king said, "No, she is too good for me." Too good or too much to handle?

Her father had to take her home, but he didn't plan to keep her. He would marry her off instead. She should make a good catch. She not only had the usual skills of embroidery, milking and cheese-making, she could read too.

Dubthach was foiled again. Brigid turned down a prize suitor, and announced she had vowed perpetual virginity in the service of Christ. She might have been contrary, but she wasn't unkind. She got a girlfriend to marry the disappointed young man.

As for Brigid, she professed her vow publicly, and founded a church and monastery on Liffey Plain. The spot came to be called Cill Dara (or Kildare) because it was graced by the shade of a giant old oak tree.

Brigid was soon joined by eager young women who admired her charity and goodness. But the church would need a priest too. She convinced a learned hermit, Conleth, to come take up the post. He ended up being consecrated a bishop, and soon a double monastery grew up under Brigid's guidance.

Monks and nuns lived separately, but gathered together in the church for Eucharist, with a wooden partition running down the center of the nave to keep them discreetly apart.

Brigid was more than abbess of one monastery though. From the legends and reports that grew up around her, it's apparent she was considered an important church leader all over Ireland.

She went out on missions of mercy and evangelization of her own, and, in turn, she housed traveling bishops and missionaries at Kildare. She loved community life, but she worked outside the walls too, among the poor, the uneducated, and the godless.

According to the legends, even nature cooperated with Brigid's generosity. Once, when she had given away all the monastery's food to the poor, her Sisters rushed in to tell her that seven bishops were on their way to visit for the night.

"Quick," she told them, "Talk to the hens and see if they will give us more eggs. Tell the trees we need some fruit, and convince the cows that more milk would be most appreciated." The bishops never ate better.

Brigid died around 524, and her fame spread far beyond Ireland, which honors her as a patron on a par with Patrick. Missionaries made her famous in England and the continent, and churches all over Europe have borne her name. Sit down at supper on Brigid's feast, February 1st, and recite an ancient grace written in her memory:

> Brigid with all virtues clad,
> Keep us free from all that's bad.
> As we sit before this food,
> Keep us safe and keep us good
> Until next we sit before
> Other gifts from God's rich store.

Move over, Newt

Much was made of the suggestion by former House Speaker, Newt Gingrich, that orphanages might offer a viable solution to today's problem of children growing up in situations which don't meet all their needs.

I'm not sure about the wisdom of the suggestion, but if more orphanages *are* built, perhaps their entryways might be graced with a portrait of the Speaker alongside a likeness of Jerome Emiliani, the Patron Saint of Orphans, whose feast is celebrated February 8.

There were indeed many true orphans in Jerome's day, children whose mother and father had both died of the plague, war or some other malady in Northern Italy in the 1500's. Jerome did what he could for them, at first working alone, then with a few friends, and finally with dozens of followers who organized themselves into the Society of the Servants of the Poor in 1534.

Jerome came about his vocation in a way that combines some of the story of Ignatius Loyola with that of Richard Nixon's aide Charles Colson. Like Ignatius, he was a soldier; like Colson, he did some jail time.

He was born into a wealthy Venetian family during a time when Venice was contending for dominance of all Northern Italy. Careers could be made in the armed forces, and Jerome pursued that route. During one of the many wars that pitted

Venice against groupings of other Northern Italian cities, he was helping to defend Castelnuovo — not too well apparently, for it fell, and he was taken prisoner.

It seems his time in the dungeons of Venice's enemies led him to consider goals other than martial glory. Prayer, penance, and perhaps even a miracle embarked him on a new way of living. As the legend goes, Mary herself helped in his escape, bringing keys that freed his fetters. These chains he is said to have hung at a shrine to Mary in the town of Treviso as a sign of his gratitude.

Jerome was not a poor man. After his return to Venice, he founded an orphanage there with his own funds. He later founded others at Bergamo and Como. The orphans were expected to learn an art or a trade and, of course, their catechism. As a matter of fact, some even say Jerome invented that venerable way of learning the faith, using the question and answer approach to religious education with his charges.

To get away from his work, Jerome would retire to a hermitage near the mountain town of Somascha in Lombardy, where he died on February 8th, 1537. Maybe he would use the hermitage to return to the long periods of prayer and penance that characterized his time in prison.

At any rate, he is remembered for his spirituality that centered on charity and service, especially to those abandoned. The Servants of the Poor eventually became the Somaschans, in memory of the place of their founder's retreat. They still serve orphans today. Children, abandoned or abused or neglected, are in as great a need as ever of friends like Jerome Emiliani.

ANSGAR, APOSTLE OF THE NORTH

It's hard to choke on pickled herring

While many seek the blessing of St. Blase on February 3rd, few may note another saint who shares that feast day with him, Ansgar, "Apostle of the North."

Ansgar was born near Amiens around 801 in what was then the Kingdom of the Franks. He was educated by the Benedictines, and eventually became one of them.

One of the more vexing questions facing Northern France and Germany at the time was what to do about the pagan Norsemen, a particularly aggressive breed of tourists who took home with them a lot more than Heineken coasters and hotel towels.

The great Charlemagne's answer had been strong fortifications at river mouths to block the raiders' entry, but weak and divided successors had let these decay.

One solution was seen in the conversion of these pagan Vikings to Christianity. An opportunity arose when the Danish King Harold found himself a fugitive in the court of King Louis the Pious. Harold was converted to Christianity and on his return to Denmark, he admitted Christian missionaries. Ansgar was one of them.

The saint seems to have achieved at least a little success on his first journey north, but returned after only a few years. Next, he tried Sweden, but could stay only eighteen months because King Louis recalled him to make him an abbot and the Bishop of Hamburg. The pope in Rome not only confirmed this appointment but named Ansgar his personal representative to all of Scandinavia as well.

From this position of strength, Ansgar made great plans for the conversion of all the Norse, even setting up a special training center for the missionaries he planned to send to them.

Unfortunately, his scheme suffered quite a setback in 845 when a Viking raiding party burned Hamburg to the ground. One hopes his earlier converts were not among the raiders.

Ansgar didn't give up. Eventually, he again made the trip north, this time as a fifty-year-old bishop instead of a young monk. He's remembered as a great preacher. This, and his personal zeal, seems to have embarked Christianity on a time of growth in Denmark. Ansgar even went on to Sweden where King Olaf, after casting lots to help make up his royal mind, decided to admit Christian missionaries there too.

Many of the Norse were indeed converted, including old Olaf, and Ansgar bears the name "Apostle of the North," or as an 1863 German biography puts it, "Apostle von Danemark und Schweden."

However, at Ansgar's peaceful death on February 3rd, 865, most of the work remained unfinished, and without the saint's leadership many of the "converted" areas lapsed into paganism.

Ansgar — a model to all who labor hard in the vineyard, but who have to leave ultimate success in the hands of the harvest master.

Apple pie and the forbidden fruit

The other day, I dripped some of my McDonald's hot apple pie into the switch box on the arm rest that controls the nine-position driver seat in my '88 Buick Roadmaster station wagon. I wasn't worried at first because I still had a lot of the hot apple pie left, and there was always the desserts on the back seat from the "Meals On Wheels" that I had forgotten to deliver.

But now, there is a burnt odor in my car and my seat has just one position — uncomfortable. I think the fire in the car must be like one of those in the deep, old coal mines of southern Ohio, slowly smoldering continuously underground. Because, yesterday, my power door locks went out, and the rear window defroster button wouldn't glow.

I wanted to chant a lament. The car was going to pieces after only 212,000 miles. But, since life has treated me pretty well so far, I'm rather short on laments. So I had to look one up.

I was attracted to that of the First Couple, uttered just after they were thrown out of the Garden of Eden for eating the forbidden fruit. In the epic poem "The Fall of Man," Eve whines:

> Well may thou upbraid me as thou dost
> O Adam, my beloved spouse, and yet
> Believe me, that thyself canst not bewail

> More bitterly the outcome of this deed
> Than I do in my heart.

And Adam, seeing her in a new light, responds:

> No heart have I
> For worship, now that I have forfeited,
> Beyond retrieve, the favour of our King.
> But let us hasten to yonder wood
> And sit within the grove's protecting shade,
> For naked as we are it is not meet
> To tarry longer here.

The lengthy poem, about 1200 lines, dates to Anglo-Saxon times, and is often attributed to a saint named Caedmon, whose feast is on February 11. St. Bede knew Caedmon when Bede was just a boy, and tells us about him in his history of the early English Church.

Caedmon lived at a time when tales were told in rhyme and song, with the storyteller often accompanying himself on the hand-held harp. This kind of entertainment was even practiced after supper in old English monasteries.

It seems Caedmon was some sort of shepherd in service at Whitby Abbey who had a problem joining in such merriment. The harp would be passed around the table with everyone taking a turn as bard. But as it neared Caedmon's turn, he would excuse himself and run out.

One night, he ran out to the stables and fell asleep. In his sleep, he heard a voice calling "Sing Me Something." Caedmon said, "I cannot sing; that is why I left the feast and came here because I could not sing."

But the voice insisted, "Nevertheless you must sing to me." "What must I sing?" the shepherd said.

"Sing about the beginning of created things."

So Caedmon began to sing. And he never stopped — hymns, poems, prayers of praise, all flowed from his tongue with great beauty and charm. Scholars even taught Caedmon Scripture and doctrine so that they could hear theology put to verse.

Caedmon became a full-fledged monk, and the abbey halls resounded with his high, clear voice for years on end until the very night he died. He asked to receive the Eucharist and to be forgiven by any he had wronged. He forgave any who had wronged him, and went to take his place in the heavenly choir.

The pope's bones and the Slavs' alphabet

Near the Colosseum in Rome lie the remains of an ancient basilica dedicated to the third pope after Peter, Clement I. If one descends through the newer church to the original or lower church, you'll see the usual frescoes, statues and crumbling niches, *and* a small plaque placed there by Todor Zhivkova, Chairman of the Bulgarian Communist Party. Why the plaque?

It all has to do with two Greek brothers chased out of Moravia by "Pilatian" German bishops, but saved by a pope's rib bone which they had found in the Black Sea while on a trip to visit Turkic horsemen who turned out to be Jewish.

The brothers are known to us as Cyril and Methodius. They were two of the seven children born to a noble Greek family over a thousand years ago. Their father was a government official in Thessalonika, who had learned the language of the Slavs so that he could deal with these immigrants who had moved south into the Byzantine Empire in Greece.

It appears he passed on a strong love of the Lord, of learning, and of languages to his sons for both became noted scholars and linguists, and, eventually, missionaries. Cyril became a priest and famed professor known throughout the empire as the Philosopher. The older, Methodius, served as governor of a province and later as the abbot of an important monastery.

Then, in 862, the Byzantine emperor told them he had a

special job for them. A Slavic prince whose territory bordered German Bavaria had sent word to both the pope in Rome and the emperor in Constantinople requesting missionaries be sent to further introduce his people to Christianity.

The pope was slow to respond, but the emperor was aware that the brothers knew Slavonic, and he thought they would make excellent candidates for the task. He was sure they could even translate the Scriptures into the language of the Slavs.

But there was one catch. Slavonic didn't have an alphabet, and there were some sounds in the language that the Greek alphabet couldn't convey. To Cyril, the solution seemed obvious. He simply invented an alphabet, one that's still used in much of Eastern Europe and Asia today.

The brothers began translating the Gospels into Slavonic as soon as the alphabet was complete. Then they headed north to begin their work in Moravia, preaching to the Slavs in their own language, and showing them how to write it.

What's more, centuries before Vatican II, they translated the prayers of the Church so that the Mass could be said in a language the people would understand.

Then the German clergy stepped in. They wanted Moravia to be tied to their hierarchy and not to a separate Slavonic church. They protested to the pope that these Greeks from the east were infringing in Western territory, and that the only proper languages for Church purposes were Hebrew, Greek, and Latin.

Cyril probably didn't help matters by calling them "Pilatians" after Pontius Pilate who had those three languages used on the inscription nailed to Jesus's cross.

The brothers had to journey to Rome to see if the pope would approve of their methods and their ingenuity. He was obviously impressed with their learning and dedication, but the decision hung in the balance until they brought forth the bones of the fourth pope to present as a gift to the one hundred fifth pope.

They had found them years before when they were sent as political and religious ambassadors from the Byzantine emperor to the Khazar tribes living north of the Black Sea along the Volga River. The Khazars did enter into a political alliance with the emperor, but their nobles chose to retain the Judaism they had already been converted to years before.

Cyril did not live long enough to enjoy his victory. He died in Rome on February 14, 869. Methodius had to return to Moravia alone to continue their work.

Eventually, the German clergy pushed the Slavonic clergy out of the area after Methodius died, but the Slavonic alphabet and liturgy spread south and east until it covered vast territories.

Cyril and Methodius ended up being important enough in Slavic culture to win the gratitude even of a Bulgarian Communist Party Chairman. In the Church, they are often called the "Apostles to the Slavs."

And Pope Clement's bones? What were they doing way over in the Black Sea? Well, that's a whole other story.

SEVEN SERVITES

They moved to the woods but never saw Snow White

The Church of the Annunciation in Florence is skipped by most tourists to that beautiful city nowadays, but for ages pilgrims were sure to gather there on March 25th because the Feast of the Annunciation marked the beginning of the Florentine year. They even left behind life-size statues of themselves, carved in wax, to mark their visit to the shrine. The statues were hung from the rafters or seated around the foyer — kind of like relatives who visited too long.

The Church became well known in Italy because of a legend that a mural of the Annunciation began there by a monk was finished by an angel. Less well known is its connection with seven Florentine merchants who began its construction in the 13th century.

Building such a church was not their initial intention. As a matter of fact, they originally left Florence to escape the political and religious upheaval of the age. They sought to live simple lives of penance, denial and service, and thereby save themselves and others. They left behind family, careers and possessions in a pious reaction to what they saw as the imperfections of Church and society. When their location just outside the city was seen as still too contaminated, they withdrew further into the hills.

The seven founders of the movement were joined by others, and gradually, after much prayer and reflection, they left the life of seclusion behind in order to serve more openly. They moved back to the city and began the construction of the church that would eventually be called Santissimi Annunciata. They formed an official religious order in 1256 under the name of the Servants of St. Mary, and became respected throughout the city for their lives of holiness and caring witness.

Bonfilius, Alexis, John, Benedict, Bartholomew, Gerard and Ricoverus can perhaps be seen as models for those who try to reform institutions from within. Others of their day were set on more radical paths. Such were the Cathari who were active in Northern Italy at the time. This sect of the "pure" saw the world as divided between realms of good and evil with everything material being part of the latter. The "most pure" renounced meat, sex, and most of the Old Testament, and scorned the worldliness of the Church. Unlike the seven Florentine merchants, they saw no hope for internal reform, and even resorted to assassination of opponents. Church and State united in crusade and inquisition against the Cathari, and they eventually disappeared from the scene.

The followers of the Seven Holy Founders however still labor today as the O.S.M.'s or Servites. There are 150 priests and brothers currently working in the U.S. The Church celebrates the feast of the original Seven Servites on February 17th. They may not have whistled while they worked, but surely they chanted in unison in their houses of prayer.

CONRAD PIACENZA

We live
in
perilous
times

Ask not for whom
The bell tolls.
It didn't toll for me —
Recently.

In a rather unnerving incident last week, I saw a very distinguished looking lady get shot at Taco Bell. She was standing in line right behind me when a teenage cook walked out from the kitchen area to talk to her older friend working the cash register.

The teen had been squirting sour cream into the burritos, and she continued to absent-mindedly pump air into her spray gun. I looked down, and my worst fears were realized. The safety was off.

Everything after that is a blur, but I remember the cashier asking me if I would like to try their chicken taco just as the teen turned toward me with her weapon. I yelled "Duck!" Then I dove to the floor. As the cashier said, "Sorry, no duck, just chicken," the lady behind me got it square in the face.

A poor peasant of Piacenza made the same mistake. He was in the wrong place at the wrong time.

He had chosen to gather sticks for his hearth right at the edge of a brush fire that was destroying crops for miles around. When a mob of furious farmers happened on the scene, they seized him and accused him of starting the conflagration. He was pronounced guilty and sentenced to death. It looked like his bell had been tolled.

But a nobleman arrived just in time with a sound defense for the peasant, his own confession. It seems Conrad of Piacenza had been out earlier in the day pursuing his favorite pursuit — wild game. He wasn't satisfied with what his beaters could scare up for him to shoot at. So he had them set fire to a whole hunting area to drive his dinner toward him.

The trick worked great, but unfortunately, the fire didn't know when to stop. It spread to fields, orchards and villages all around until Conrad took fright and ran home. All his serfs kept quiet. It was only when Conrad heard of the peasant's sentence of death that he came forward.

Conrad wasn't threatened with death. But by the time he had made restitution for his foolhardiness, he had spent not only his own fortune, but all of his wife's dowries as well.

All this caused Conrad to rethink his values, and his wife changed her life's direction as well. He became a hermit, and she entered the Poor Clares.

Like many hermits who wished to remain entirely alone, Conrad was continuously pursued by people who heard what a good hermit he was, who sought him out for advice and blessing. Many miracles are attributed to this saint whose feast is on February 19, but all he ever wanted was solitude.

He moved from Piacenza to the area around Rome, and then to Sicily, where he relocated deeper and deeper into the mountains to be alone with his God. He was buried in the church of St. Nicholas in remote Noto sometime around 1365.

The lady with the sour cream dripping from her chin took advantage of the confusion to ditch me in line. So much for good manners.

MARGARET OF CORTONA

Was
Margaret
of Cortona
a lousy
mother?

Margaret sat by the window and watched. Arsenio should have been home yesterday. She waited and waited, but he didn't return.

They had been lovers for nine years. He had promised to marry her, and had repeated the promise many times. It had given her hope. Their son would inherit Arsenio's estates. Her father would perhaps speak to her again, and she could finally hold her head up high — no longer just a mistress, but the lady of the castle.

Arsenio didn't return that night, but his hound did, whining and whimpering looking cold and hungry. The dog barked and dragged at her skirt until she followed it into the woods.

There, under an oak tree, just barely covered by leaves and dirt, lay the dead Arsenio, stabbed over and over again. Who had done it?

Margaret never tried to find out. In that moment of horror or grief or panic, which one we can't be sure, an immense change came over her. She started on *her* road to sainthood, a life of penitence and prayer.

In her new state of mind, staying at the castle was unthinkable. She left the trinkets and baubles behind, took her son by the hand, and went home.

But her father wouldn't keep her. She had run off with the handsome nobleman, disgraced him and his second wife, and now he insisted Margaret would have to leave.

39

She had heard that the followers of Francis of Assisi helped repentant sinners. So she headed for Cortona to look them up. The rest of her story is the stuff of legends.

She was taken in by kind ladies who introduced her to Franciscan spiritual directors. These friars encouraged her in her desire to repent but warned her against excessive mortification and abasement.

Eventually, her spirit of sorrow and remorse gave way to a greater spirit of love and service. She nursed the poor, founded a hospital, consoled the grieving, and counseled the perplexed. She dreamt mystical dreams and experienced holy visions. She fasted and prayed, and prayed and fasted, and communed directly with God. By the end of her life, her witness had outlived her reputation, and even vicious gossips came to admire and respect her.

Folks flocked to her grave, and a church in her honor was built at Cortona. She was canonized in 1728 and given a feast day on February 22nd.

But something about Margaret is troubling. What about the boy? In her time of perhaps self-hatred, did she maybe hate him? Did she see him as some kind of outgrowth of her sin, some poisoned fruit that itself had to be cleansed?

Her biographers agree that in her years of begging for the poor, he was given the poorest portion, next to her own, of whatever she received. He survived, grew to manhood, and joined the Franciscans himself. But his childhood was one of imposed sacrifice and renunciation. Was it fair for Margaret to include him in her life of penitence?

The French novelist François Mauriac attempts an answer. Margaret was madly in love with God, he writes. Such a love doesn't mean, though, that human blindness and errors disappear. Love is love. Wisdom is wisdom.

The Crusader who never left home

Near the border of Iran and Iraq is a place called Manzikert. Over nine hundred years ago a Moslem Turkish army there smashed the forces of the Christian Byzantine Empire. The emperor in Constantinople eventually appealed to the pope and all Western Christians to come to his aid, save his empire, and recapture Jerusalem and other cities the Turks had overrun.

In that same year that planted the seeds for the Crusades, Peter Damian was off on a crusade of his own — his last.

Peter had been born sixty-five years before in the very town he was headed toward, Ravenna in Italy. He was on a mission from a reforming pope to bring his hometown back into allegiance to Rome. He succeeded, but on the way back he died on February 21st, 1072.

Surely Peter's parents never foresaw his importance as a papal emissary. Otherwise they would not have abandoned him to die as one of too many heirs to afford. He was saved, ironically as it turned out, by the "wife" of a parish priest who cared for him until his parents regretted their rather radical form of estate planning.

Still, they died when he was very young, and his upbringing was left to older brothers. His youth was hard with little emotional warmth or support, but he did receive a sound education, and eventually became a respected teacher himself. He was respected, but probably not popular.

Peter would be happiest as a hermit priest, strict with himself and preachy toward others, striving for perfection, for complete chastity, for a holiness to be found in prayer and reflection, in withdrawal from the temptations of the world.

He got his chance for all of this when he entered the hermitage of the Holy Cross at Fonte Avellana. As a matter of fact, he was so enthusiastic in these pursuits that he soon became prior there and advisor to all churches and monasteries in the area on the vexing subject of "reform".

Peter's strictness, his sermonizing, his condemnation of imperfections may seem harsh, but they stemmed from the state of the Church in his day. Priests who were vowed to celibacy often had wives; bishops were frequently installed by secular powers who needed them as sources of revenue and royal control; monasteries had in many places become known more for their material treasures than for their spiritual wealth; and clergy of all ranks were paying to get ordained.

Like prohibitionists on Bourbon Street, Peter and other reformers had a lot of work to do. Corruption among the clergy was even causing people to doubt the worth of the sacraments that priests administered. Peter preached the need for change, and took his message to the emperor in Germany, the pope in Rome, and to everyone who would listen. Mostly, though, he wrote... and wrote, and wrote and wrote. Sermons, letters, exhortations, poems, inspiring biographies, tracts and treatises all poured from his pen, enough to make him a Doctor of the Church.

On the one hand, he condemned abuse. But, unlike other reformers, he still reassured the faithful that unworthy ministers could not hinder the power of God's grace channeled to them through the sacraments of the Church. He did all he could to encourage the goal of a moral and educated clergy. He waged his own war, not against the infidel at the gates, but against infidelity within. Would he call himself a Crusader? The last lines of his poem on the glories of heaven read:

> Christ, the Palm of worthy warriors,
> when my shield is laid aside,
> Bring me to Thy heavenly city,
> there forever to abide.
> Grant that I, the veteran's bounty
> with Thy faithful may divide.
> Strength supply in heat of conflict,
> ceaseless struggle to maintain.
> Grant Thy servant, his warfare ended,
> well deservéd rest to gain.
> Grant that I, Thyself deserving
> may Thyself as prize attain.

GABRIEL POSSENTI

Watch it, Sarge, the monk's packin'

While other European nations had grown into united monarchies or republics, Italy remained a collection of small kingdoms and provinces, many ruled by foreigners. Giuseppe Garibaldi and other nationalists were determined to change all that.

Garibaldi had had to flee Italy after an unsuccessful insurrection in Genoa. But he gained valuable military experiences while abroad. He led armies in Brazil and Uruguay, and earned such fame that Abraham Lincoln would later offer him a command in the American Civil War.

In 1859, the Kingdom of Piedmont was supporting Garibaldi in his efforts to unite Italy by force if necessary. This meant capturing towns and territories from the pope, foreign rulers, and native princes.

Unfortunately, Garibaldi's "platoons of passionate patriots" often behaved more like brutish brigands. A small group of about twenty of them once chased off the local militia of a little hill town called Isola, and proceeded to loot and burn the place.

One of the guerrillas grabbed a young woman and was dragging her from her house with God knows what intentions when he was confronted by an angry young seminarian, Gabriel Possenti.

Gabriel told the man to let the woman go, and when he refused, grabbed the soldier's own gun from its holster and pointed it directly at him. *Then* the man saw the error of his ways and released the lady. When another soldier rounded the corner of the house, Gabriel disarmed him too.

Then, a pistol in each hand, he began taking prisoners one by one until he ran into a stubborn, drunken sergeant. There was a standoff. Would the soldier drop his weapon or open fire? Would the seminarian have to shoot?

A rather unlucky little lizard chose that moment to dart across the dusty street. In the wink of an eye, Gabriel aimed and fired. The lizard stopped and flopped, the wide-eye sergeant dropped, and the guerrillas left Isola to look for easier pickings.

The monastery's rector came out of his room where he had locked himself in with all the church's valuables, and the townsfolk gathered around Gabriel to cheer his courage.

Where did he learn to shoot like that? In high school and college. Gabriel and his buddies had always loved to hunt, and he was considered the best marksman among them. They thought him the best dancer too, giving him the nickname "Il Ballerino."

They had all enjoyed good times going to the theater in Spoleto, and showing off to the girls there by racing their horses along its cobbled streets.

But Gabriel had a serious core beneath his good looks and fun loving humor. His mother and his best loved sister had both died while he was growing up, and he considered life so important that he wanted to do something he thought special with his.

Over and over, he had asked permission to join the Passionists, a religious Order that combined something of contemplative seclusion with a missionary apostolate. His father eventually gave in, and thus Gabriel's presence in Isola when Garibaldi's men hit town.

He became as popular among his brother Passionists as

he had been among his college friends. So they were all stricken as word spread of Gabriel's declining health. He had contracted tuberculosis. Dizzy spells, coughing fits, painful headaches all eventually confined him to his bed.

He ended up cheering everybody who came to cheer him, and he faced death with the same courage with which he had faced the sergeant. He never achieved his goal of ordination to the priesthood, but gained the admiration and respect of everyone who knew him. He died on February 27, 1862 at the age of 24.

JOHN OF GOD

The rigors of Lent

I'm still stuffed from fasting on Ash Wednesday. I knew I had a big day ahead of me when I got up. So I ate a hearty breakfast of pancakes, fruit, cereal and toast. I sailed through a busy morning.

At lunch, I really was not very hungry, but I wanted to stop in the school cafeteria on pizza day to say Hi. I ate one large square of pizza. Then, it was brought to my attention that there were a lot of leftovers since the kids don't eat as much cheese pizza as they do pepperoni pizza.

All the adults were helping. So I did my part and ate three or four more squares.

After evening Mass, I realized my mistake. Supper has always been my main meal ever since I was a child. Ash Wednesday supper though would have to be huge to be bigger than the sum of my other two meals that day.

Fortunately, Stouffers makes a party size tray of macaroni and cheese that's pretty good. It took me till 10:00 P.M. to finish it, but then I was able to sleep the sleep of the just, knowing I had complied with all the rules of the Lenten fast.

My mortification may not have impressed John of God, however. He *really* knew how to do penance, especially after he got out of the insane asylum.

Of course, John had a lot to do penance *for*. In *Saint Watching*, Phyllis McGinley aptly terms him "a gambler, drunkard and mercenary." John fought both Frenchmen and Turks while he was in the army of Emperor Charles V and had other adventures in Africa, Portugal and Spain.

Eventually, a feeling of remorse began to overcome John as he matured. He started looking for some deeper meaning to his existence. Providentially, he was in Gibraltar handing out cheap religious pamphlets when the great preacher John of Avila came through town.

John of God was so convinced by Avila's preaching of his need for repentance that he went through the streets beating his breast and asking everyone for mercy. He was put away as mad.

Avila came to visit him, though, and convinced John to cease all the lamentations and to channel his remorse into a more constructive direction. John of God calmed down and set to work.

He rented a small house in Granada and began gathering the ill and the poor to give them some relief from their sufferings. He also started to gather helpers who eventually became the numerous Brothers Hospitallers of St. John of God.

John's example of loving service impressed all who knew him and great miracle stories are told about him, such as the one in which he rescues all the patients from a fiery inferno in one of his hospitals, going back and forth through the flames repeatedly without suffering so much as a blister.

Even John's death provided a model of courage and sacrifice. It came about from a fever he contracted after jumping into a river to save a drowning man. John was just 55 when he died on March 8, 1550.

DANIEL RUDD

As African-American history month and Catholic Press month come to a close, Martin Luther King and Daniel Rudd come to mind. They never knew each other. King was only four when Rudd died in 1933, thirty five years before King's own death in 1968. Many remember that King was assassinated in Memphis in April, but it was in February in Atlanta that he had preached about the kind of eulogy he would like spoken over him. The Scripture reading for that day had been about the disciples arguing over who would sit at Jesus' right hand when he came into his kingdom. King said:

"Yes, Jesus, I want to be on your right side or your left side, not for any selfish reason. I want to be on your right side or your best side, not in terms of some political kingdom or ambition, but I just want to be there in love and in justice and in truth and in commitment to others, so that we can make of this old world a new world." Because of what he died for, King is included in many lists of Christian Martyrs. But the original call of the martyr was to witness to Christ in life. So perhaps Daniel Rudd can be placed on some lists too.

Rudd was born into slavery in Bardstown, Kentucky. Catholic families in the South did indeed own slaves, as did Jesuits in Maryland, Sisters of Charity of Nazareth in Kentucky, and even Archbishop Carroll and Bishop Flaget. Many Catholic masters saw to the spiritual needs of their slaves, being sure they were baptized and arranging for them to get to Mass, but they shared their neighbors' moral blindness to the intrinsic evil of the "peculiar institution."

After the Civil War, Daniel Rudd moved to Springfield, Ohio to go to high school. In 1886, he published a newspaper called the *American Catholic Tribune*. It editorialized that the Catholic Church would be a great home for African-Americans because of its universal nature, reaching out to so many people of such different backgrounds across the world. He defended the Church's doctrine, and encouraged all to become familiar with Pope Leo's XIII's encyclical *Rerum Novarum*, and the social teachings of the Church.

At the same time, he saw the weakness and limitations of Catholicism in America. He decried the lack of educational opportunities for African-Americans even in parochial schools, and protested against demands for segregation in the Church.

He was the driving force behind three national congresses of African-American Catholics — each calling for the Church to be the true champion of justice, racial equality and education for all. He repeatedly professed his faith in the Church and at the same time called upon it to live up to its own best ideals.

Rudd wanted a Church that fully accepted African-Americans on equal terms, unions that did not discriminate on the basis of race, and decent housing for all working people. His hope and confidence in Catholicism never waned. He wrote, traveled, spoke and organized to achieve real justice. At times he gained helpful allies like Archbishop Elder of Cincinnati, but he also ran into outright derision and polite patronization.

Unlike King, who died in the prime of life, Rudd lived till he was seventy-nine. What's white and black and red all over? A Church holy and universal, but embarrassed by its human weakness and imperfection.

> **Did you not know I must be about my mother's work?**

After having five girls, my parents proceeded to have six boys. This meant that we could attempt some stunts smaller families could only dream of, such as having brother "A" jump from the shoulders of brothers "B" and "C" on to one end of a homemade teeter totter, thus launching brother "D" up and back off the other end into the waiting arms of brothers "E" and "F." Except that the launch, like an early Atlas missile, went sideways so that brother "D" landed face first in the waiting gravel of the alley behind our house instead.

Little Katie Drexel never had that much fun. They only had girls in her family, just three of them.

As the heirs of Francis and Emma Drexel, the wealthy girls did manage to enjoy themselves though: parties, balls, rides around the country, vacations all around America, and even the grand tour of Europe and a private audience with Pope Pius IX.

The pope and Katie's father Frank traded hats. They had met years before when he was on his honeymoon, Frank that is, not the pope.

But there was a serious side to the girls' upbringing too. The family had a tradition of public service and social action to uphold. Frank Drexel's father had been Treasurer of the German Hospital, and Mrs. Drexel's father, Michael Bouvier, President of the French Benevolent Society.

Mrs. Drexel was herself a one woman Catholic Social Services of Philadelphia before such an institution was even invented. Drexel banking profits made her generosity possible, but Emma's involvement with the poor was personal.

She aided them right out of her mansion at 1503 Walnut Street, and hired the city's first Catholic social worker to help her. The poor were visited in their homes and given a ticket to see Emma Drexel on one of the three days each week she devoted to her work.

She would see each one privately and try to respond to their needs immediately by giving them "order slips" for what they lacked. Grocers, coal companies, landlords, shoe stores all honored Drexel order slips.

But Emma wasn't just kind. She was organized and sharp too. Finding jobs for her clients was always a priority, and she expected full value for her expenditures. When a carpenter charged her $7.50 for a pauper's coffin she knew usually went for $5.00, she made him adjust his price.

Emma Bouvier Drexel had a name for her operation: Dorcas. In the Acts of the Apostles, a certain lady of Joppa named Dorcas was known for her good works, her charity to the poor, and her sewing of coats and garments for the needy.

Katie and her two sisters were required to help their mother with Dorcas, and to give some of their spending money to that charity. Emma Drexel couldn't introduce her girls into the highest circles of Philadelphia society. She may have been rich, but she was Catholic and an immigrant. She and Frank introduced them to something far more important though: personal justice, charity, and service to the poor.

When Emma died in 1883, it was discovered that she was quietly paying the rent for over 150 families. Each of her daughters in some way continued her mother's work. Katie of course grew to be Mother Katharine Drexel, founder of an Order of Sisters dedicated to serving Native and African Americans.

She started up Xavier University in New Orleans and founded almost 50 missions and schools around the country. Blessed Katharine Drexel lived to 96, and spent over twelve million dollars of her own inheritance in her work. She died March 3, 1955.

Along with her millions, did Katharine physically inherit some call to holiness from her mother Emma? Impossible. Emma Bouvier Drexel was her stepmother. The inheritance was purely spiritual.

FRANCES OF ROME

Her greatest miracle was in an '88 Fiat

Only one thing is scarier than speeding along twisting mountain roads in Italy. That is speeding along twisting mountain roads in Italy with a moving van chasing you. Our driver had offended the van driver by employing his Third Rule of Mountain Driving: Rule One — heavy fog setting in, drive faster; Rule Two — dangerous curve ahead, drive faster; Rule Three — a yield sign on the right, drive faster.

We finally lost the truck driver in the hilltop town of Perugia. The coward wouldn't go down the street that became a steep set of steps. Everyone was amazed that we survived the stairs, and I was thoroughly surprised that the lady carrying the fruit could jump so high. There was no likeness of St. Christopher on the dash, but a tiny statue of Frances of Rome, patron saint of motorists.

When she was eleven years old, Frances wanted to become a nun. One husband, three children, two plagues, a war and three popes later, she got her wish — sort of. Her parents would not let young Frances enter the convent, but instead arranged her marriage into another wealthy and noble Roman family. All reports confirm that she was a wonderful wife and mother, personally seeing to the rearing of her children and hosting her husband's many social gatherings in their family palace.

But Frances also worked outside the home. She and her

sister-in-law left the palace almost every day to visit the poor in the slums and hospitals of Rome to help feed and nurse them. At first, the care of her own children caused Frances to cut back on her outside activities, but then history intervened to make her work even more important.

While Frances was balancing the work of wife, mother and social worker, the Church in 1410 was split into factions that recognized one of three opposing popes, the one in Rome whom Frances's husband supported, and others in Avignon and Pisa. Religious disputes often became entangled with political disputes, and supporters of the various claimants to the Chair of Peter didn't shrink from resorting to arms. When one opposing group seized Rome, Frances's husband had to flee and their home was looted and partly destroyed. She stayed with her children and turned what remained of the house into a hospital for victims of famine and plague. She was recognized as a gifted healer and respected and loved by many throughout the city.

The Council of Constance was able to agree on a single pope in 1417 and what is known as the Great Schism in the Church came to an end. Frances's beloved Lorenzo returned home where they enjoyed another twenty years together. She founded a group of women dedicated to nursing the poor, and continued her own work with the needy. But it wasn't until Lorenzo died in 1436 that she was able to join her own Oblates of Tor de Specchi. Her childhood wish was fulfilled for just four years. Perhaps when she isn't busy helping tourists in Fiats, she can aid the working wives and mothers of our own day.

Bishop Sophronius

The great Omar and the holy bishop

It had been a perfect day: sunny skies, no wind and plenty of powdery snow on the slopes. Our junior high field trip looked to be a great success. Then one kid seemed to want to spoil everything.

The announcement had just been repeated for our students to turn in their skis and prepare to leave. But he shot right by me at the bottom of the hill and headed straight for the chair lift for another run.

I wasn't going to let him get away with it. I ran right over to the line of skiers at the lift and grabbed him by the back of the collar. "Oh no you don't, young man!" I told him. I dragged him backward on his skis, squirming and struggling, right up to the phys-ed teacher.

"This one thinks he can completely ignore your announcement," I said triumphantly. She looked at me only long enough to reply, "Maybe that's because he doesn't go to our school."

I felt like one of Caliph Omar's generals, scorned in their hour of greatest victory. They had just taken Jerusalem for him, and were riding to greet him in all their finery. But when the very austere and plainly dressed Omar saw them, he threw gravel on them, shouting "Begone! Is it thus attired that ye come out to meet me?"

Omar was much more impressed with the quiet holy man who came to see him. Bishop Sophronius had come to formalize the surrender of his city to the leader of much of Islam. Omar received him with quiet dignity and friendliness.

The two toured Jerusalem together. The Caliph imposed only a slight tribute on the defeated city and let the Christians worship at their shrines. He picked a site for a mosque and then returned to his capital at Medina in Arabia.

Sophronius left the area too, going to Alexandria for a couple of years before he died on March 11, 638. Some say it was of a broken heart after seeing the fall of his diocese to the Moslems. But it may have been from plain hard work.

Sophronius had tirelessly combated the Monothelites — those who said Jesus had no truly human will, and was still agitating for a council to be called to condemn the heresy right up until his death. Then there were his notable sermons to prepare and preach, biographies he worked on tirelessly, and hymns and poems as well.

St. Sophronius is remembered as a pious and good leader, one skilled in rhetoric and debate, and stubbornly faithful in his dedication to his job. Much the same can be said of Omar, or Umar Ibn Al-Khattab, who outlived the bishop by just six years.

The site he chose for a mosque in Jerusalem eventually saw the construction of the famous Dome of the Rock, or, as it is sometimes called, the Mosque of Omar.

Charlemagne's nemesis, a royal family's genesis

Charlemagne felt himself divinely called to unite Europe under his rule and to re-create the vanished Roman Empire in the West. A lot of stubborn German tribes must have been blind to his true vocation for they fought him ferociously.

One German Saxon who was a real thorn in his side, or rather in his rear, was Widukind, a tribal leader of the West Saxons.

When Charlemagne first conquered most of Saxony, penetrating far to the east, an uprising broke out to his rear in the west. It was Widukind.

When Charlemagne invaded Italy to "bring the Lombards to their senses," his own kingdom back home was raided. It was Widukind.

When Charlemagne was away in Spain, losing to the Basques and the Moors, his Rhineland was ravaged. Widukind again.

Only a will as tenacious as Charlemagne's could finally bring the chieftain to terms. After years of struggle and thousands of dead Saxons, Widukind finally came to Charlemagne's camp for surrender and baptism in 785.

That's right. Charlemagne's foreign policy included a missionary component. He saw Christianity and the Church as unifying factors in his empire. Defeated barbarians had to take on a new religion with their new ruler.

But some of Widukind's independence and perseverance must have been passed down his bloodline, for his descendants for years played important roles in the history of Germany and the Church.

One of these was St. Matilda, a noble Saxon girl who was sent away to a convent to be raised by the abbess, who also happened to be her grandmother.

Matilda grew in knowledge, piety, and beauty, but eventually wanted to leave the convent for life in the world outside. Fortunately for her, Duke Henry's wife wanted to leave him so that she could get *in* a convent. Henry hunted with his hawks so often that he was called the "Fowler." So maybe she was tired of waiting around for the old bird. At any rate, Matilda got out, Henry's ex got in, and Matilda and Henry got together.

It turned out to be a love match for 23 years. They had five children: two kings, two queens, and an archbishop that messed up their full house.

Matilda was widely respected and loved by the people, but remained in old convent habits by living simply and prayerfully. She governed skillfully when Henry was away hunting birds or enemy barons.

In 936, her life changed dramatically with Henry's sudden death. She publicly foreswore worldly power and accelerated her already generous giving to the poor and to those starting up monasteries and missions.

She was so generous that her son Otto accused her of diverting royal funds for her private charities. Instead of defending herself or asserting her rights, she left the palace and retired to the country house she was born in.

She returned twice, once to try to bring peace between Otto and his brother Henry the Quarrelsome (you can guess how far she got with the latter), and once to govern for an older and wiser Otto when he went to Italy to woo the beautiful Adelaide and to be crowned emperor by the pope.

She willingly retired again, coming full circle back to a detached and contemplative convent life, dying March 14, 968. She was buried alongside her Fowler.

BRUDER KLAUS

> But did he drive out any snakes?

Environmentalists are ruining the children.

I recently organized a retreat for about 50 seventh and eighth graders preparing for Confirmation. They were angels. They helped carry all the gear to the cabins, they listened to instructions, they participated in games and discussions, and they sang and prayed out loud at Mass.

Everything was just fine until we sat down to eat. Then, it started. The first troublemaker complained that the paper plates were too white. "Hey, Father, this paper isn't recycled. Recycled paper is more off-color." "Yeah," chimed another, "What a waste of trees."

Then a little thing with freckles and pigtails spoke up. "And why did you bring all these Styrofoam cups? That's not a renewable energy source you're using up you know." A fourth: "That's right. You could have just asked, and we would all have brought washable mugs or cups."

I shamefacedly continued to eat my lasagna while I tossed away empty soda jugs as they were passed down my way. Then, one seventh grader returning from the bathroom caught sight of all the plastic liter bottles in the trash. "Look at this! What idiot has been throwing away all this reusable plastic? Father, where do you want me to stick these bottles?"

Don't worry. A saint intervened, a great patron saint honored as the father of his country with parades, songs and festivals. I'm speaking of course of St. Nicholas of Flue, the great peacemaker of Switzerland.

Nicholas had to learn how to make peace. He had a wife and ten children. He did all right by them, supporting them as a soldier, a judge and an important politician. But once he saw that they were all OK, he pursued his second career and first love — being a hermit.

He withdrew to the valley of Ranft, a few miles from his home on Lake Lucerne. People continued to seek his advice as a retired judge, and as his reputation for holiness spread, they came to ask spiritual guidance as well. The tall and weathered looking hermit, with the long hair and short beard, came to be known as Bruder Klaus.

Tales grew up around him concerning his sanctity. One reported that he lasted nineteen years at Ranft without food or water, subsisting solely on the Eucharist. Other stories celebrated his wisdom as a counselor and arbitrator.

Thus, when the Confederation of Switzerland was about to break into pieces, an appeal was sent out to Bruder Klaus to save the day. It seems that the three urban cantons, Lucerne, Bern and Zurich, allied themselves against the five rural cantons of Switzerland, and sought to add two more cities to the Confederation.

Alarmed at this threat to the balance of power between city and countryside, the rural Swiss were ready to go to war to protect their interests. But before the country could shatter into violence and bloodshed, with everyone pulling out their army knives, calmer heads prevailed. A conference was called at Stans in 1481 to sort out complaints and accusations.

The Swiss didn't get anywhere though until someone thought to send for the hermit and sage, Nicholas. He talked the urban and rural cantons into dissolving their treaties against one another and making a new treaty to include all eight of them and the two new cantons as well.

Switzerland was saved. Bruder Klaus returned to his solitude, and died at the age of seventy on his own birthday, March 21. His feast is celebrated on that day everywhere except in Switzerland, which honors him on September 25.

Which way to the St. Rutilio parade?

On March 17, Irish-Americans and others around the country will be on the march. Some will be marching to honor the day. Others will be marching to protest that they were not allowed in the march to honor the day. Still, others will be marching to protest the protest. Many will end up in some of the same places, eating Italian pizza and drinking green German beer.

It's very fitting that the root cause of all this marching did a lot of marching himself, all over Ireland, spreading the Christian faith. More than just preaching Christianity, though, Patrick is important because he organized Christianity. He set up over fifty bishops in dioceses around the island, had many churches built and helped small communities of brothers and nuns get established.

It was this work of organizing Christians that got Rutilio Grande killed.

The prophets of the Old Testament frequently reminded God's people that they were called to justice, not just to fairness and honesty, but to a burning desire to uphold the rights of the poor and oppressed. The New Testament portrayed Jesus as one "chosen to bring good news to the poor... to proclaim liberty to captives... and to let the oppressed go free." The Church has understood and applied these revelations in evolving ways throughout its history.

For the last 100 years, it has seen itself called to help build a more just world. After Vatican II and the writings of John XXIII and Paul VI, theologians and Church leaders in Latin America began developing an understanding of Christianity's relationship to the world called liberation theology: people are called not only to be liberated from sin, but also to help liberate one another from any condition that threatens the dignity of the human person — created in God's image and redeemed by Christ.

In the largest diocese of El Salvador, liberation theology coincided with Church efforts to reach more and more peasants with fewer and fewer priests. The idea was to divide parishes of thousands into Christian base communities where mobile clergy would train lay leaders to catechize, to explain Vatican II, and to lead Bible study groups. The result was the rise of a new lay leadership from among ordinary people, and a basic change in the role of religion in their lives. Many peasants came to see the faith not only as a solace in this "vale of tears" but also as a reminder of their worth and dignity as human beings — equal in baptism to the wealthiest landowner.

Father Rutilio Grande was a pastor with 35,000 parishioners, most working on sugar cane plantations they didn't own. With a few other Jesuit priests, he divided the parish into 25 zones and trained over 300 lay leaders. It's doubtful he intended political involvement, but it was only a matter of time before peasants convinced of the Church's preferential option for the poor and of their own worth began to act together to resist years of economic and political dominance by a wealthy oligarchy. Many leaders of base communities became leaders in labor and land reform movements.

In turn, some of the ruling elite saw Grande and priests like him as subversive. Right-wing forces made grave threats. On March 12th, 1977, Father Grande was on his way to celebrate Mass with one of his base communities when shots rang out from a cane field near the road, killing the priest and an old man and young boy traveling with him.

The diocese's brand new bishop was Grande's friend. Oscar Romero saw Rutilio's death as proof that he would have to resist government efforts to silence or control the Church. Peasants in El Salvador sing:

> The God of the poor is angry
> at seeing so much injustice,
> For God's will is that each should receive
> wages to match his labors.
> Rutilio, a prophetic voice,
> preached love to the four winds
> but the hatred of resentment
> armed the hand of an assassin.

It may never replace "When Irish Eyes Are Smiling," but surely the Irish oppressed for years themselves recognize the sentiments.

BENEDICT OF NURSIA

When God and his sister made him break the rules

Fifteen popes and folks claiming to be the pope have taken the name Benedict, including the Sixth who was strangled by the brother of his predecessor, the Eleventh who was poisoned by a French nobleman, and the Fourteenth who was "elected" by the vote of just one cardinal present. The other twelve fared considerably better, but why so many Benedicts in the first place?

It's probably because Benedict of Nursia, who preceded them all, has consistently enjoyed the devotion of a grateful Church for almost 1500 years.

A Roman nobleman from the area around Spoleto, Benedict found himself disgusted with how immoral life in Rome had become.

So it appears he experimented with being a Christian hermit in the caves of the Abruzzi region at a place called Subiaco. Soon, he became so good at prayerfully living alone that people came to visit and imitate him, which meant of course that he could no longer prayerfully live alone.

Some hermits over at Vicovero begged Benedict to come be their leader. He went, but he didn't stay long, and it's not quite clear why. Some sources say he found out the hermits wouldn't really follow any leader, and others say he found out a few of the hermits were trying to poison him. Perhaps the two explanations are connected.

At any rate, his notoriety became such that more and

more Christians flocked to him until he decided to take some in permanently. First, he founded twelve small monasteries of twelve monks each, and eventually the famous, large monastery at Monte Cassino in 520.

Of course others had founded monasteries before, but Benedict's lasting contribution would be the development of his Rule, a small book of instructions on just how life would be lived at Monte Cassino and later at other monasteries he would found.

His rule became the norm for practically all of monasticism in Western Christianity. His instructions show the temperament of a classical Roman mind. The monks would live lives of balance and moderation, with appropriate times set aside for work, prayer and study.

Their day would be organized and disciplined, but not wildly ascetic. They would not fast themselves into sickness or beat themselves into purity. Instead, they would pursue less concern with self and greater love of God through practicing Christian virtues, studying their faith, and obeying their abbot.

If they had a little wine along the way, some decent food, and eight hours of rest each day, no problem. Benedict felt one hemina (half a pint) of wine per monk should be enough, but his Rule #40 said the abbot could issue extra if "the circumstances of the place, the work, or the heat of summer necessitates."

A favorite story about this famous lawgiver concerns how his sister and God got him to break one of his very own rules.

His monks were not to stay away from their monastery overnight. So on his yearly visit to see his sister Scholastica, he presumed he would be back before nightfall like he had been for years and years.

But Scholastica felt that the aged brother and sister might

not see one another again, at least in this lifetime, and begged him to stay over to continue what might be their last visit.

Rules were rules though, and Benedict got up to go. Scholastica prayed, God threw some thunderbolts around, and a violent storm raged all night. Benedict stayed and talked through the night.

Sure enough, three days later Scholastica died. Benedict lived on until March 21st, 547 when he was carried in to die in the church of his beloved Monte Cassino.

The area is still interesting to visit, and the Abruzzi wines are delicious. If you ever get there, drink just one hemina in Benedict's memory. Of course if the work of touring has exhausted you, or the day's been too hot, there is always good old Rule #40.

CHAPTER II

Turibius de Mongrovejo

In 1532, Francisco Pizarro and two hundred Spaniards came to Peru. They killed the emperor of the Incas; they killed the warriors who rose in fury against them; and they killed one another. They kept killing one another until Pizarro's chief lieutenant, the Spanish viceroy, Pizarro's brother, and Pizarro himself were all dead. In the meantime, hundreds of thousands of Indians died too, chiefly from smallpox, measles, influenza and typhus, European diseases to which they had no immunity.

Fifty years after Pizarro, a very different kind of Spaniard arrived in Peru, Turibius de Mongrovejo. He did not want to be there.

He had been a noted lawyer and chief judge of the Church court in Granada when news reached Spain of the death of the bishop of Lima, Peru's new capital. King Philip II wanted him to go take over. Turibius thanked him, but pointed out that he wasn't even a priest, much less a bishop. For a king who could launch an Armada of over 100 ships not once but twice, this small impediment presented no real problem. Turibius was ordained a priest, consecrated a bishop, and shipped out to the New World all in record time.

Philip knew he needed a strong and able leader for the Church in Peru. As biographer Sean Kelley describes it, Lima was populated with too many "Spanish landlords crazy with greed, Spanish soldiers crazy with blood lust, and Spanish clergy just plain crazy."

Turibius found his huge diocese a wild and untamed place. Many settlers were out to make their fortunes as fast as they could, even if this meant violence, oppression and exploitation of native workers on large estates or deep in silver mines. A lot of the clergy competed with other colonists to get ahead.

Turibius used his authority to confront officials and landowners alike. He headed the diocese for over 25 years and did succeed in halting many abuses. He tried to serve the poor as best he could, founding hospitals and shelters. He even began a seminary so that some better educated clergy might set a moral example, and he learned Indian dialects to preach to the natives about Christ.

He is said to have confirmed St. Martin de Porres, and met St. Rose of Lima when she was still a little girl. While visiting her home village in the mining district, he explained to her and her brothers and sisters that the colonists owed a grave debt to the Indians because they had taken their land. He felt the only just repayment was to bring Christ to them. He told the children, "All your lives you must remember that we who live in Peru will not be pleasing to God if we forget the Indians. We must be just to them, and kind, and in that way we'll teach them to love God." At 68, he was journeying into the Andes to visit Indian villages when he died on March 23rd, 1606.

CADOC

I'll race you to the well, sweetheart

The great Welsh saint, Cadoc, had four-teen aunts and uncles who were saints too, including Aunt St. Keyne. It's said that Cadoc once struck the hard ground for her so that a spring would flow forth to nour-ish her in her declining years.

Before Keyne died, she blessed the spring which became known as St. Keyne's Well. Newly married Welsh couples used to race to the well after their wedding ceremony because it was believed that the first one to drink from its waters would be the real master of the house.

As interesting as Cadoc and his various aunts and uncles might seem though, it's his parents who are truly fascinating. They were bandits.

Cadoc's father Gwynllyw was a chief among chiefs in South Wales. He fell in love with the beautiful Gwladys, but her father would not hear of a match. So Gwynllyw took mat-ters into his own hands. He gathered together 300 of his kins-men, rode to Gwladys' home, and the couple eloped. What a ladder that must have been.

Gwladys' family was taken by surprise, but soon recov-ered and organized themselves to give chase. At this point, the story becomes cloudy. Either Gwynllyw's men fought off Gwladys' family on their own, or they had help from none other than King Arthur himself. Some even say that Arthur too fell in love with Gwladys, and that it took several knights of his round table to talk him out of stealing her for himself.

At any rate, Gwynllyw and Gwladys did wed, and did have a son whom they named Cadoc. It appears they also roamed the countryside living off the land and grabbing what they could. Cadoc is credited with getting his parents to mend their ways, but a vision Gwynllyw had also may have helped.

Alban Butler quotes an angel as telling Gwynllyw he was to retire from the highways and byways to live the life of a hermit. His vision, mysteriously, was in the second person plural. So he took it to include Gwladys too.

> The king of heaven calls and invites you...
> I will show you the way you must walk to obtain
> God's inheritance. Lift up your hearts and do
> not imperil your souls for what is perishable.
> By the river's bank and on rising ground there
> stands a white steer. There is the place of your
> habitation.

So Cadoc's parents dissolved their gang, separated, and chose isolated spots for each to live a life of prayer and meditation. They must not have been too strict a pair of hermits though, because Cadoc visited each of them often and had to scold them for meeting to skinny dip together in the River Usk.

Records of Gwladys' death are unclear, but Cadoc's father called for him in his last days, and had the pleasure of holy communion and Cadoc's company at the end.

Cadoc founded a monastery at Llancarvan around the year 500, and also journeyed across the channel to Brittany in northwestern France. He could not stay there though — too many pirates. He returned to Wales where the fame of his wisdom and sanctity drew others to him. Not surprisingly, Cadoc has a recognized Welsh feast day on September 21st. But so does Gwynllyw, on March 29th.

JOHN CLIMACHUS

> **Fall off the wagon and you might fall off the ladder**

Within a few hundred years after Christ, some of his followers saw themselves as called to live their faith through a rigid discipline over mind and body, apart from the concerns of everyday living, apart from the world, apart from family, apart from marriage. Their motivation was both negative and positive. The world was to be avoided because it tempted one to sin. The mind and body had to be controlled for the same reason. On the positive side, if a person could so completely detach himself from world and flesh, his spirit could more easily and directly commune with God. He would achieve a one-to-one encounter with the creator. Augustine admired their search: "Think of this encounter, seizing, absorbing, drawing the witness into the depths of joy. Eternal life would be like this moment of understanding."

Men who pursued this "moment of understanding" came to be known as monks, those who live alone. Actually just a small percentage of monks truly lived alone: the anchorites. Many more lived in communities that sometimes numbered in the hundreds: the cenobites.

Either kind of monk could go to the extreme of seeing the world and the flesh not as mere distractions of the spirit, but as real enemies to be resisted or literally whipped into shape. Their eccentricities provide the strange tales about the monks who flagellated themselves until blood flowed, or the hermit who purposely built his cell so tiny that he could never stand up or lie down, or the one monk who bragged that his fasting made him look more like a corpse than anyone else.

They should have listened to John the Ladder Man. John was sixteen in the year 600 when he came to join the monks at Mt. Sinai. Over 50 years later, they insisted he become their abbot. Both his own monks and those in other monasteries admired the wisdom and holiness John seemed to have gained both in solitude and in community. So they asked him, like a new Moses, to share the vision he had on Sinai of the monk's way to God.

In response, John wrote *The Ladder of Divine Ascent*. His book became so influential throughout all of Eastern Christianity that he became known in history as John Climachus from the Greek word for ladder.

In roughly 200 pages, John described the monk's journey to God, to true holiness, as consisting of thirty steps, like the rungs of a ladder, one for each year of Christ's life before his baptism in the Jordan. The monk began his climb to God by first practicing certain virtues such as obedience to a spiritual director and a continuous calling to mind of the death of Jesus in his behalf. Further along the climb, the monk would have to struggle against dangerous passions or vices like malice or slander or drunkenness.

If he applied himself, he could eventually attain the higher virtues: simplicity, humility, discernment. When he became truly detached from the cares of the body, when he finally saw himself as completely empty, God, who is love, could fill him up. The monk would then be truly in love with God.

John's ladder is not an easy one to climb. He felt it was not for all believers, but for monks who wanted to be a shining example to those living out in the world. He avoided advising the somewhat eccentric behavior described earlier. Instead, he cited brotherly love and humble obedience to a good spiritual guide as the monk's best guarantee for success. The contrast he drew was not between spirit and body, between God and the world, but between redemption and the fall, immortality and corruption.

He wrote with much common sense and a good understanding of human behavior. He also wrote with some wit and humor as a few scattered steps from his ladder suggest.

Eggs warmed in dung hatch out.
Unconfessed evil thoughts hatch evil actions.
Galloping horses vie with each other.
A zealous community encourages individual zeal.
A man who has heard himself sentenced to death will not worry about how the theaters are run.

His feast is celebrated March 30th.

Hit the road, Holy Father

Few saints can claim to have chased the pope out of town. Vincent Ferrer is an exception.

The tiny hilltop town of San Gimignano is noted for its fourteen sturdy stone towers that rise like skyscrapers over the humble roofs of their neighbors. The towers look picturesque but also odd and out of place, being so skinny and so tightly packed together in little San Gimignano. So imagine how the town must have looked in the Middle Ages, when it had seventy-two of them.

The towers started to rise as protective refuges for warring families divided along political lines in strife torn Italy. After a while it became a fashion statement to have the tallest tower in town. The fourteen towers remain as a reminder of the precarious nature of political involvement in 14th century Italy.

It's understandable therefore that when a Frenchman was elected pope in 1305, he decided to "dally" a while before making his journey through territory where a fifty-foot tower marked the corner of one's yard instead of a white picket fence.

So Pope Clement led the church of Rome from Avignon, about 700 miles away by the coast road. Six more popes followed his example until Gregory XI came to the eternal city in 1378. When Gregory died, the college of cardinals went into conclave to elect a new pope. There were eleven Frenchmen, four Italians, one Spaniard, and a mob of screaming Romans outside insisting on an Italian pope who would stay in Rome. The election took just two days, and an Italian archbishop became Pope Urban VI.

At first it looked like things had gone well. Urban was known as a reformer, and had an excellent reputation regarding his upright life. Unfortunately, he was also bad-tempered, tactless, and utterly intolerant of less moral Church leaders. Some of them, in turn, thought he was downright crazy, and the cardinals who elected him began to doubt the wisdom of their vote.

In May, the cardinals met again, away from Rome, claimed the mob had swayed their vote, and "un-elected" Urban. Clement VII took the title pope and, along with the cardinals, promptly went back to Avignon.

For the next thirty-seven years, there were two and sometimes three people claiming to be pope. Vincent Ferrer, a Dominican priest, was the advisor and confessor of one of them at Avignon, Benedict XIII.

He had been called there from his native Spain because his talents as a preacher, teacher and retreat master were being praised everywhere. He preached to thousands and visited individuals. He moved in lofty social circles, but he was also known for his care for the poor. And, he was recognized as a gifted healer of the sick and the alienated. His greatest joy though seemed to lie in reinvigorating lax Christians.

He didn't stay at Avignon long. It seems the pope who wanted him as an advisor, didn't want his advice, which was that Benedict seek reconciliation and some sort of understanding with his rivals. The saint even became ill over the stress of Church scandal and discord.

He eventually got permission to leave, and flourished once again on a teaching and preaching journey that took him to towns all over Europe. As Vincent's fame grew, so did the importance of his opinion as to who was the rightful pope. Even King Ferdinand wanted to know.

Ferrer had concluded that Benedict's stubbornness was harming the Church, and that unity could never be restored with him in the way. He returned to give the pope one last sermon before a huge crowd, and shouted out just what he thought. Benedict left town.

The Council of Constance deposed Benedict, and got two other popes to resign, and Vincent Ferrer returned to the work he loved best.

As he aged, he became so feeble that he had to be helped into pulpits, but once he got rolling into a good sermon, he was his old eloquent self, God's herald to a sinful world in need of grace and moral reform. He died on April 5th in Holy Week of 1419.

BERTHOLD

Rules are rules

A lot of the talk about the priest shortage in the U.S. has centered on concern about having enough priests in the future to celebrate weekend Masses. What a lot of people haven't realized though is that the shortage has already become crucial in the area of witnessing marriages.

As fewer and fewer priests are asked to witness the marriages of more and more Catholics, scheduling nightmares have ensued. One way pastors are dealing with the crunch is the establishment of stricter guidelines as to whose marriage they will witness.

Our parish, for example, has some specific requirements. The parents of the bride or groom must be registered in the parish, attending Mass regularly, supporting the church financially, and volunteering in at least some capacity.

Thus, I had to tell one prospective bride last week that I wasn't sure I could schedule her wedding here. I explained, "Your parents don't appear anywhere in our parish listing. I can't see any sign of support from them all through 1996, and they don't appear on any listing of readers, ushers or communion distributors."

"But, Father," she replied, "I'm seventy-six years old. My parents have been dead for years."

"Well, I can certainly sympathize with your situation," I told her, "but rules are rules. If I start making exceptions for all kinds of cases, I'm going to get protests from others I've turned down."

"But couldn't you just explain to them, Father, how I've been head of the Altar Rosary Society here for ten years, and that I've been the housekeeper here in the rectory for forty-five?"

"Well I suppose I'll have to, won't I, Clara? But I just know I'm going to catch a lot of flack on this one."

St. Berthold would never have given in so easily. He was a stickler for rules, especially those governing the monks from the West living on Mt. Carmel.

Legends once held that there were actually Old Testament monks on Mt. Carmel in Israel from the time of the prophet Elijah. Some historians dispute that idea but agree that certain bands of prophets in the area might have lived some kind of communal life similar in some ways to monks of the Christian era.

We have better evidence concerning monks on Mt. Carmel dating from the time of the crusades. Both a Greek monk named Phocas and a Rabbi of the same era talk about crusaders from the West turning into hermits sometime before 1180 and settling on the holy mountain associated with Elijah.

One of these was a gentleman named Berthold who seems to have gathered some scattered hermits from around Palestine into a small community of maybe a dozen. Once they came together, they followed a common rule enforced by Berthold: each monk was to stick to his own cell or hut except for times of common prayer or work; all fasted and abstained, living lives of seclusion and quiet prayer, and everyone was to seek perfection in withdrawal from the temptations of the world.

They didn't get to stay on their mountain long though. As defeated crusaders withdrew from Palestine, the Carmelites followed in their wake to become much more numerous and widespread throughout Christendom. Berthold, who some would call their founder, has a feast on March 29th.

As Clara was leaving my office, she stopped to ask what the usual offering was for a priest at weddings. I knew I had her then because I had picked up a great line from a priest friend for just such an occasion.

"Oh, the offering for the priest is completely voluntary," I told her. "But some give him about the same amount that they pay to the florist."

"That will be fine then, father. My little green house won the Spring show again. So I'll bring all the flowers I need from home."

The cardinal, the priest, the bishop and dead Peter

For three years in the 1950's, Stefan Cardinal Wyszynski, the primate of Poland, was imprisoned by its communist government. Upon his release in 1956, he promptly resumed his resistance to the anti-Church policies of Party Secretary Wladyslaw Gomulka.

The cardinal had to fight for permission to build churches, and for enough paper and ink to keep Catholic publications going. He struggled with five communist regimes in a row, and Solidarity's Lech Walesa was always welcome at his home.

So was a young priest name Jerzy Popieluszko. He was a chaplain to the steel workers of Warsaw's mills. At a Mass in April of 1983, he preached to steel workers from all over Poland on the need for a greater awareness of God in their lives, and in the life of their union, and on their calling to nonviolently resist godlessness.

Within two years, he was dead, abducted and murdered by government agents. Both the cardinal and the priest were aware, I'm sure, that they had a very special patron in their struggle against unjust rulers in Poland: Stanislaus Szczepanowski, or St. Stanislaus, Bishop of Kraców.

Stanislaus became bishop in 1072 by the will of the people and the approval of the pope. Right away he came into conflict with Boleslaus II, Poland's ruler at the time.

Boleslaus has been called the Bold for his courageous independence from the Holy Roman Emperor and for his holding of Kiev. He might also be called the Lecherous, though, and it was this trait that brought matters to a head with bishop Stanislaus.

Everybody else was afraid to confront Boleslaus with the evil of his kidnaping of a nobleman's wife so that he could have her as his own. But Stanislaus denounced the sinner to his face.

Infuriated, the king brought charges against the bishop accusing him of having swindled a now-deceased landowner. The king got the dead man's nephews to swear the bishop never paid for the land.

But the bishop got the dead man to swear that he did!

The deceased's name was Peter. As the trial looked to be going very badly for the bishop, he could be heard praying aloud for help until Peter himself walked into court in his grave shroud, testified he had indeed been paid, and walked back out. Boleslaus was unimpressed though and continued his public sin until Stanislaus had to excommunicate him.

The enraged king ordered his men to attack the bishop in a small chapel outside the city where he was praying, but the troops were too afraid. So the king did it himself, hacking the bishop to pieces. They didn't call him Bold for nothing.

Stanislaus was almost immediately seen as a martyr, and was recognized as patron saint of Poland. His feast is April 11th. Boleslaus lost his kingdom, and died in exile in a monastery where he had gone to do penance for his sins.

All you can eat on Wednesdays

Wednesdays at the college seminary were one of the better days in the "good old days" of the Church. Students were always in an upbeat mood because they would be leaving the seminary grounds in the afternoon to do apostolic works around town — tutoring, teaching catechism at the orphanage, working in the inner city, and so on.

The rector and chief linguist was in an even better mood, however. He and an old friend always went fly fishing on Wednesdays. They relished the sport, even designing and tying their own flies; and morning Greek class would sometimes be interrupted by elaborate explanations of imaginary casts into flowing streams. I wonder if the rector and his friend ever prayed to St. Zeno.

At the edge of the oldest part of the city of Verona stands the Basilica of St. Zeno, a beautiful Romanesque church over a thousand years old. Inside, St. Zeno is sculptured in painted marble, seated on a bishop's throne, and holding a shepherd's staff or crozier. Dangling from the crozier is, of all things, a small fish. Zeno loved fishing in Verona's River Adiage, and is the patron saint of anglers.

He had other interests too: combating heresy, training his priests, founding convents, and, most importantly, preaching to his people. Although he lived before 400 A.D., over ninety of his sermons have been preserved, and they tell us something about the saint and about the concerns of the Church in his day.

Chief among the latter was the challenge of Arianism, a fourth century heresy that denied the divinity of Christ. The Council of Nicea condemned Arianism in 325, insisting that Jesus is "true God from true God, begotten not made." But it took years of preaching by bishops like Zeno, and a few executions by emperors like Theodosius, before the Nicene Creed (the one prayed at Mass) won overall acceptance in the empire.

Zeno also stressed that his people might be a little less joyful and rowdy at the agape meals that followed services and a little more joyful and hopeful at funeral Masses. Convinced of the resurrection to come, he asked them to quit interrupting funeral liturgies with their loud laments and moans.

He didn't always nag though. He complimented his beloved Veronese on their kindness and generosity, telling them no one in Verona, living or dead, ever went about naked thanks to their neighborliness.

Zeno's feast is celebrated on April 12th. His bones lie in the crypt of the church that bears his name. The restaurants in the neighborhood serve great fish. Go on Wednesdays for the "all you can eat" special.

BISHOP ABDAS

Fiery Bishop Abdas inflames the world

The first policeman who stopped me last Sunday was very polite. I found myself locked out of the house, and walked around the side of the place to try to get in. I had asked the lady who lives down the alley to call the police if she ever saw anyone trying to climb in any of the windows facing her way. I took it for granted she understood that didn't mean me.

I was drooped over the window sill, halfway in, when I heard the siren coming down the alley, and a shouted command, "Freeze!" "Don't shoot!" I yelled back. "I live here."

"I know, Father," came the reply. "I recognized the shiny seat of your black dress pants from way over here. But the box you're standing on is about to tip over. So I didn't want you to move."

After the officer steadied the box, I was able to get my lower half in the opening. I thanked him, and he said, "No problem. But, for security reasons, you ought to lock these windows along the alley." "Oh no you don't," I said. "Then the next time I try to get in, you'll arrest me for breaking and entering."

He walked away with a puzzled look on his face.

Bishop Abdas of Persia should have practiced such caution when dealing with the worldly authorities of his day. Instead, he was downright rash.

The King of Persia, Yazdegerd I, had begun his reign with

a policy of toleration toward the minority Christians in his realm. He took a lot of criticism from his nobles for his moderation, but he was able to counter with the argument that such a course kept the peace with the Christian Roman Empire to the west of Persia.

Bishop Abdas must have forgotten the bloody persecutions carried out by the king's father and grandfather against the Christians, because, in 420, he burned down the Temple of Fire, a major Persian shrine.

A furious Yazdegerd demanded the Christians rebuild it. Abdas refused, and an even more furious Yazdegerd launched a persecution that lasted well beyond his lifetime — 40 years to be exact.

Abdas was one of the first to go, and Christian churches all over Persia were destroyed. One believer caught up in all the turmoil was a certain Benjamin, a deacon of the Church. He was arrested, beaten, and cast into a dungeon.

The persecution must not have been absolute, however, because a representative of the king visited Benjamin after the deacon had spent a year in prison. The ambassador reported back to the king that Benjamin promised not to preach about Christ in public, and the deacon was released.

But, either the ambassador was mistaken, or Benjamin went back on his word, because as soon as he was freed, he boldly preached about Christ to all who would listen.

He was arrested again, and, this time, tortured. Benjamin died from his torments around the year 424. His feast is celebrated March 31st. Rome and Persia went back to war partly as a result of Bishop Abdas' boldness.

PETER ABELARD

Now you see him. Now you don't

Peter Abelard died in the South of France on April 21, 1142. It might be a while before he's declared a saint.

Abelard was already a popular and famous professor at Notre Dame in Paris when his landlord asked him to give private lessons to his intelligent and lovely niece, Heloise. Unfortunately, the lessons became too private. They fell in love, had a son, and got married, but secretly, in order to protect his career as a rising young cleric destined for greatness in the Church.

The uncle was enraged at first, but seemed to go along with the arrangement until he mistakenly thought Abelard had sent Heloise to a convent as part of a plan to get rid of her.

Uncle Fulbert arranged for an attack that left Abelard beaten and physically mutilated. There was no longer any question of the lovers staying together. Abelard felt he had been punished by God "in that part of my body in which I had sinned." He decided to become a penitent monk, and insisted Heloise join the convent where he had hidden her away.

A story of unguarded lust and brutal violence? Yes, but also a tale of a great love and perhaps an even greater conversion.

Abelard and his wife met from time to time in formal settings at the convent Heloise headed as abbess. He wrote hymns for her nuns to sing, and together they even compiled a collection of their love letters and religious correspondence. The letters portray a reserved but caring Abelard, and a more passionate but completely chaste Heloise. If only his dealings with the rest of Christendom could have been so tranquil.

Abelard offended fellow monks by criticizing their laxity and by using rational analysis to belittle some of their favorite misconceptions about their history. Then he failed as a hermit when eager, young students insisted on searching out the famous teacher. Finally, he troubled the Church itself with his critical and questioning approach to doctrine, especially in the areas of Christ's role in salvation and the true nature of sin.

Still, the influence of his writings and his fame as a teacher continued to grow until he was summoned to a meeting before the king, assembled bishops and that great defender of Christian orthodoxy, Bernard of Clairvaux. Abelard wasn't fearful, he knew he could best Bernard in dialectical debate as he had many others who had been victims of his keen intellect.

But there was to be no debate. Abelard's questionable teachings were simply read out loud, pronounced heretical, and condemned. He refused to accept the prearranged verdict and took off for Rome to argue his case before the pope himself.

He never got there. Somewhere along the way, he had a change of heart. Was he just tired or ill, or broken in spirit? Or was he finally over an intellectual pride that made him seem truly arrogant to humble minds?

At any rate, for the first time in his life perhaps, he quietly listened to some kind of advice, that of Abbot Peter who had given Abelard refuge at his monastery at Cluny. Peter convinced the great teacher to humbly send a profession of faith to the pope, emphasizing his true orthodoxy.

At the same time, the kindly abbot got the pope's agreement to a plan where Peter would quietly retire there at Cluny.

Abelard was accepted, loved and at peace. In his final letter to Heloise, he writes:

> My sister Heloise, once very dear to me in the world, and now dearest in Christ. I would not be called a philosopher if it denoted any error in the faith. I would not wish to be Aristotle if that should separate me from Christ.

The good abbot did Abelard one final favor after his death. Heloise had always hoped that her dearest would be buried at her convent where she hoped to be buried too. But Peter's monks at the monastery where Abelard had spent his last days had gotten to so venerate the great teacher that they wouldn't let the body go.

What was the saintly abbot of hundreds of Benedictines to do? He had the body swiped.

POPE PIUS V

There's Ghislieri. Hide the cards

Pope John Paul II has access to more fancy church vestments than Imelda Marcos had shoes. So why is he so often seen in a plain, white cassock?

The answer has to do with Antonio Ghislieri, a poor shepherd boy who grew up to become a Dominican friar, then a bishop, and eventually Pope Pius V.

Antonio assumed the papacy at a crucial time in the history of Catholicism. The Council of Trent had labored in three different sessions over the course of eighteen years to reform some of the abuses in the Church that had led to the Protestant Reformation.

All kinds of decrees had been issued. But would they be carried out? Popes Paul IV and Pius IV had begun the work, but a lot remained to be done when the latter died in 1565.

The reformers, led by Charles Borromeo, knew the man whom they had chosen to succeed him, for Ghislieri was known to be tough, honest and hard working. He would see that Trent had lasting effect in the Church.

As Pius V, the one time shepherd did not disappoint Borromeo and his friends. Bishops were made to reside in their dioceses and not govern from afar. Folks receiving incomes from Church offices were made to actually do the work they were paid to perform.

Convents and monasteries were forced to live by the rules of their spiritual founders, and the Vatican court itself became more sober, prayerful and respectable. The pope personally set the tone by dressing in a simple Dominican habit of white, a color scheme maintained to this day.

The prayers which clergy were to recite each day were standardized in a new Breviary, and precise instructions on just how to say Mass were included in the Roman Missal. A catechism was issued for parish priests to use in instructing believers of all ages, and abuses in the issuing of indulgences were cleaned up.

In short, no one could criticize the dedication, honesty and vigilance of Pope Pius V. And much of his work remained unchanged until Vatican Council II. However, there were those who had cause to fear him. In his dedication to heaven, he was hell on Protestants, Jews, free thinkers, and Sunday gamblers.

The Protestants he chased out of Italy entirely and attempted to get them arrested in other lands too. He tried to expel all Jews from territories under his control, and he used the Inquisition and the Index of condemned books to stifle heresy and dissent. For good measure, he excommunicated England's Queen Elizabeth I.

In all this though, he seems to have been morally consistent. In his mind, all of the above, like those who gambled on the Lord's Day, were untrue to the True Faith as he saw it. And he was determined to purify and defend the Church against all challenges from within and without.

St. Pope Pius V lived to see his reforms well under way, dying at age 68 on May 1, 1572.

HILDEGUNDE

Clothes don't necessarily make the man

If someone calls you a bollandist, relax. Unless they are a Carmelite, it's probably a compliment. In 16th century Antwerp, Jean Bolland and a few other Jesuits organized themselves into a society for the critical study of the saints and their relics. They wanted to use historical analysis and careful research to separate fact from fiction, myth from reality.

In an age that boasted at least 23 heads of the 12 apostles and enough chunks of the true cross to open a lumber yard, they had their work cut out for them.

Nevertheless, they plunged ahead with great vigor and insight, publishing volume after volume of the *Acta Sanctorum* over a two hundred-year period, right up to the time of the French Revolution.

They were not universally appreciated. They had to defend themselves against the Spanish Inquisition at one point, and they made many enemies among the Carmelites for insisting that the Old Testament prophet Elijah could not have been their founder.

Keeping in mind then the integrity and scholarship of the bollandists, it's important to note that *they* believed the incredible story of Hildegunde of Schonau.

Hildegunde's father was either a knight or a merchant of a small town along the Rhine around 1180. When the knight's (or merchant's) wife died, he decided to go on a pilgrimage to the Holy Land. He took his only child Hildegunde along.

The knight (or merchant) died on the way home, after entrusting Hildegunde to an untrustworthy companion who robbed the twelve-year-old's money and took off. Hildegunde journeyed as far as Verona where the youth was almost hanged, not once but twice — once by the authorities who accused Hildegunde of robbery, and once by the real robbers after the child was released.

Surely Hildegunde was relieved to finally reach Germany, relieved but nonetheless penniless. The youth chose the option of entering a Cistercian monastery at Schonau as a lay brother. Hildegunde found acceptance and support, and, as Brother Joseph, became known for quiet prayerfulness. Perhaps the novice had had enough adventure for one life.

Brother Joseph got to enjoy the monastery life for only a few years, dying in 1188. The novice told a nursing monk the exciting story of a life of travel and peril, but left out one small detail that was only discovered after death. Brother Joseph should have been called Sister Josephine. Ever since her father had embarked on his pilgrimage, she had worn her hair short and dressed like a man.

Given the dangers of travel for all pilgrims, much less undefended young girls, Hildegunde would probably not have survived otherwise. Nor did she have many choices after she got home. Without family, without dowry to impress either a groom or a convent, Hildegunde was trapped. The Cistercians were still a young and reforming group. Many other monasteries and convents accepted only the children of those able to endow the order.

Like courageous women of every age, Hildegunde made hard choices in difficult, and often unjust, situations. She is honored for that courage on April 20th, the anniversary of her death as Brother Joseph.

La Popolana and her reluctant babbo

Where's the pope at home?
Today the answer's Rome
But once there was a chance
Our response would have been France.

From 1309 to 1376, seven popes led Catholicism from the town of Avignon along the Rhone in what is now southern France. Clement V was bishop of Bordeaux when he was elected pope. He got as far as Avignon and settled in to stay. His six successors, fearful of the violence that racked Italy, and under hospitable pressure from the French, decided they liked Avignon too.

Christians in the rest of Europe complained about too much French influence on what was supposed to be a universal Church. One who complained very loudly and effectively was Catherine of Siena. The basis of her complaint was not any special training in canon law or dogma, not any privileged position as part of a princely family, but something far weightier — personal encounters with Christ.

Catherine's visions began when she was very young and continued all her life. Sometimes they uplifted and enlightened her; sometimes they were sources of awe and fright.

Were they real? Certainly her friends thought so. They looked to a lively and engaging Catherine for guidance and direction. Though she was barely over 30 when she died, much older people had long respected her wisdom and common sense. She possessed penetrating intuition, and may even have been clairvoyant.

She had originally considered her visions merely as paths to her own salvation. She retired alone to her room for years of contemplative prayer. There she says she learned that "there is no perfect virtue — none that bears fruit — unless it is exercised by means of our neighbor."

So she emerged from her self-imposed isolation, from her small cell in her parents' house, to nurse victims of plague; to advise and entertain a growing circle of devoted disciples; and to counsel prelates and princes on their responsibilities to God and God's people. Among the happiest at this turn of events had to be Catherine's parents. With twenty-three other children they doubtless needed the space.

Some contemporaries thought Catherine and her visions rather strange, others even called her bewitched, but most considered her saintly and rather fun to boot. They named her La Beata Popolana, the Blessed Girl of the People.

What theology she knew she probably learned from her Dominican confessor Raymond of Capua. But like other mystics, Catherine had a more direct path to the knowledge of God. It depended not on doctrinal theology or on biblical revelation, but on an overwhelming awareness of the intimate presence of the Other in the mystic's life. The mystic, in a sense, became totally immersed in and directed by the indwelling love of God.

Being directed in person by God of course gave the mystic some very firm opinions about what should be going on in God's Church. Catherine expressed these opinions in hundreds of letters, several to Pope Gregory XI in Avignon, whom she called her dad or Babbo. Encouraging an indecisive Gregory to return the papacy to Rome, she wrote: "Dear Babbo, sweet Christ on earth. All you need is grit, determination, and a real hunger for the salvation of souls."

Eventually, she made the trip to Avignon to add personal pressure, and Gregory gave in. Later, Catherine was called to Rome to advise Gregory's successor Urban VI on his zealous, though ill-tempered, reforms of the Church. She died there of a stroke on April 29th, 1380.

She reports on many of her visions and ecstasies in her *Divine Dialogue*. Speaking of entering the presence of Christ in mystic union, she writes:

"The more I enter, the more I find, and the more I find the more I seek of Thee. Thou art the Food that never satiates, for when the soul is satiated in Thine abyss it is not satiated, but ever continues to hunger and thirst for Thee."

ATHANASIUS
OF
ALEXANDRIA

"...nor disputatious bishops"

Around 350 A.D. a Roman nobleman complained that the imperial mails were running later and later because too many bishops were clogging the roads going back and forth to council after council after council.

What were all the councils debating? They were arguing whether Jesus was really God. Some bishops said yes. Some said no. Some said kind'a.

The trouble had begun about twenty-five years earlier with an Egyptian priest named Arius. He had proclaimed that Jesus was created, not eternal, and so was not on par with the Father. In an age and place that took doctrine very seriously, these were fighting words.

The followers of Arius set their beliefs to music, and heretical songs could be heard in marketplaces, dockyards and even barracks all around the eastern Mediterranean. Orthodox Christians responded with hymns of their own, and soon both sides were banging out notes on their opponents' heads.

The Emperor Constantine may not have fully appreciated the doctrinal subtleties involved, but he knew public disorder when he saw it. He summoned the bishops of his empire to a council at Nicea. Over 300 attended. After much learned debate, and a lot of pressure from the emperor, they agreed that Jesus was "begotten not made, one in being with the Father." Or at least it looked like they agreed.

Actually, a number of the bishops remained unconvinced, and without Constantine's august presence they wavered in their support of the Nicene Creed. Sometimes, succeeding emperors favored the Arian viewpoint, so that even orthodox bishops went soft on Arianism.

One that never faltered though was Athanasius of Alexandria. He became bishop there in 328. Had he joined the circus instead, he could have stayed home more. As it was, Athanasius was exiled or on the run at least five times over the next 45 years. He is described as a small man, but wiry and tough as nails, in both mind and body. He needed to be.

His was the voice of orthodoxy. In letters to popes, in audiences before emperors and councils, in the cathedrals and streets of the empire, he insisted on the divinity of Jesus. When his opponents couldn't challenge him on theological grounds, they charged him with bizarre crimes ranging from breaking a chalice to murdering another bishop. Sometimes his only supporters were the monks of the Egyptian desert who hid him for years when his life was at grave risk.

Disagreement and disunity among the Arians, a very orthodox Emperor Theodosius, and a clearer exposition of the nature of the Trinity, all led to the eventual triumph of the Nicene Creed. Arian bishops were forced out of office once and for all, and Athanasius was restored as bishop of Alexandria to live out his final years in peace.

His intellect helped saved orthodoxy. His craftiness helped save his life. Once when he was on the run up the Nile, Athanasius' boat was overtaken by some soldiers who asked him if he had seen the criminal Athanasius. In saintly honesty he answered, "He is very near." The soldiers shot past him then rowing even faster in their pursuit. His feast is celebrated May 2nd.

GREGORY NAZIANZEN

"Take
this job
and..."

Gregory had never wanted to be the bishop in the first place. So losing the job in 382 didn't bother him that much personally. But he admitted he would dearly miss his people. They had been through some tough times together.

Gregory had come to the "true" Christians of Constantinople just a few years before when they were a despised minority harassed by the Arian Christians then running the Church there.

The Arians felt Christ was not timeless but had been created by the Father, while Gregory insisted Jesus was "begotten not made, one in being with the Father." Those who prayed the Creed that way didn't have a church to pray it in in Constantinople. So they met in a house on the outskirts of the city which Gregory called the Anastasia, or Church of the Resurrection.

Orthodox leaders had encouraged him to take up the precarious post of bishop to the little group so that if an anti-Arian Emperor should come to the throne, they would in Gregory have the right man in the right place at the right time.

He had already been consecrated bishop of a small diocese in Asia Minor, a fact which had pleased his father since he had been a bishop too in Gregory's home town of Nazianzus. (Married bishops were still accepted then.)

Sure enough, when Emperor Theodosius took power in Constantinople, he kicked out the Arian bishop and gave the cathedral and the other churches of the city to Gregory's care as the rightful leader.

Gregory lasted less than a year. Church politics, doctrinal wrangling, and most especially his own desire for peace among God's people led him to resign. He said, about the bishopric of the greatest city in Christendom, "This dignity I did not desire. I assumed this office much against my will... I am ready to depart."

Thus, he might have passed into history as a relatively unimportant figure — except that he loved to preach and people loved to hear him. He was so highly regarded as a preacher that his orations were published right after his death. We still have forty-four, but there were once many more.

These long sermons and his dozens of letters or epistles so influenced Church leaders and theologians over the years that he has been called both a Father and a Doctor of the Church, titles reserved for just a handful in history.

In retirement, Gregory turned to other writing he loved to do, poetry; 16,000 lines of it as a matter of fact. Professionals in the field say it's mostly very bad. One calls his stuff "the most wearisome of monotonies." Another, commenting on his lengthy poem on *Admonishing a Virgin*, comments, "If Hercules could have read it, he must have rested in the middle."

St. Gregory went to his own rest in 390. His feast is celebrated May 9th. For all you virgins out there, eight lines out of his 210:

> Thou journey'st well but haste
> Behind is fiery waste!
> Take to thy steps good heed
> And to the mountain speed;
> Cast not one backward glance
> On Sodom — lest perchance
> Thou, fixed upon the ground,
> A pile of salt be found.

None of his lyrics were successfully set to music.

PACHOMIUS

> If no one sees your hair shirt, does it do anybody any good?

When Bishop Athanasius of Alexandria was on the lam — running from imperial authorities, he was able to hide for years among the hundreds of monks and nuns of the Egyptian desert. The fact that he had so many hiding places to choose from, and so many folks to conceal him, was due in large part to his friend Pachomius.

Pachomius had been a young Egyptian pagan when he was drafted into the army around 300 A.D. He was miserable. Poorly paid and underfed, he felt army life was not for him. Once his mood was brightened though when some Christians came to visit his troop while the soldiers were being transported along the Nile.

The kindly visitors offered food, encouragement and prayers. Pachomius did not forget this experience, and when he left the army, he became a catechumen — one seeking to enter the Church. He not only became a member, but he ended up leaving a lasting impression.

Pachomius left the pagan world behind just as some Christians were leaving the whole world behind. As Christianity grew in size, was practiced more openly, and made adjustments to life in the empire, some believers saw it as becoming too contaminated by the world around it. They chose to live holier lives by withdrawal into prayer, fasting and penance practiced all alone. They became the hermits of the desert areas. In their solitude, many grew in wisdom, holiness and insight, being sought out as spiritual guides. Others just grew weird. It may have been due to their excessive asceticism, some eating only grass, or it may have been caused simply by the stress of living entirely alone.

Pachomius tried this kind of life for about six years before coming up with a different idea: growth in holiness did not have to take a solitary path. As a matter of fact, communal life too could be a way to salvation. As St. Basil once asked, "If you live alone, whose feet do you wash?"

Pachomius began gathering groups of monks and nuns into monasteries that eventually housed hundreds which dotted the Egyptian countryside all around. Prayer and fasting were still important, but the former would often be recited in groups and the latter would not be too extreme. There was no meat on the table in his monasteries, but nobody had to live on grass either. The communal table boasted bread, fruit, cheese and vegetables, and sometimes even fish.

Pachomius' Rule that he established for his monks and nuns also called for manual labor in service to the community and for the study of Scripture. When the monks weren't praying together, they would mumble quiet prayers while farming, baking, weaving and cooking, all in behalf of one another.

Eventually such monks numbered in the thousands, and could be counted on to defend the orthodox like Athanasius, or to set an example of brotherly love to the rest of the Church, or even to provide the nucleus of a good mob when a pagan temple needed burning.

Pachomius' ideas moved west and the organization and tradition of monasticism there owe much to his influence. The monastery's goal was seen as the salvation of the monk, but in Europe, it also ended up being a center of learning, a storehouse and reproduction factory of ancient manuscripts, an agricultural school, an inn for travelers and pilgrims, and sometimes even a hospital.

The shape of Western civilization would look somewhat different without monasticism, and monasticism would indeed look different without Pachomius. Who, for example, would ever go to Gethsemane to taste their grass? The saint died in May of 348, and his feast is celebrated on the 9th.

Divine mercy Sunday

I don't think that the second policeman I ran into last week was very observant.

After he pulled me over, he asked, as they sometimes do, "Do you know why I stopped you?"

"Well," I said, "I may have been going over the speed limit, but I thought going faster would be safer since I was coming up on a curve in the road while I was passing that third car."

"No, that wasn't it."

"Then maybe I threw gravel on you when the car swayed over onto the berm? But I can explain that since a glob of mustard just fell out of the bottom of my sandwich and I was trying to clean off my pants with this bottled water here, and took my eyes off the road just for a second to see if there was going to be a spot."

"No, that wasn't it either."

I could tell that he was upset that he had missed so much. So I decided to skip the part about the ostrich. Instead, I just told him I wasn't sure why he had stopped me.

"Your thirty-day tags have expired. This van isn't legal."

"Oh," I said, "I realize that, but I'm on my way to get the van inspected by the Highway Patrol for our safety sticker so that we can license it as a Church bus. The tags just expired before I could get all the safety repairs done on it."

"These tags expired October 26th."

"Well, I wasn't worried about that since it was parked on private property the whole time, and I figured there was no hurry because I thought the Highway Patrol was going to come to my house to inspect the van."

He looked at me like I was crazy. I'm sure of it. I've seen that look before. But he must have been in a merciful mood, because he let me go.

On the Second Sunday of Easter, Catholics here and there around the world implore for mercy on a deeper level. They pray what is called "The Chaplet of Divine Mercy." The chaplet is a series of prayers prayed on rosary beads.

On the beads normally reserved for the Hail Mary, for example, the following is said: "For the sake of His sorrowful Passion, have mercy on us and on the whole world."

Advocating such a prayer used to be illegal.

A Polish sister by the name of Helen Kowalska, or Sister Faustina, claimed in the 1930's to have had a vision in which Christ called for greater mercy to be practiced by his followers in word, deed and prayer.

An inner voice taught the chaplet to Sister Faustina who recorded it and other visions and instructions in her diary. A Polish priest who escaped his war torn country in 1940 brought the devotion to the United States, and others took up the special prayer.

The Holy See at first outlawed "the spreading of images and writings advocating devotion to the Divine Mercy in the form proposed by Sister Faustina." But after he came to the Chair of Peter, the former Archbishop of Kraców had the issue reexamined.

Sr. Faustina's chaplet is now widespread in the Church, and its use encouraged by the Association of Marian Helpers out of Stockbridge, Massachusetts. And the late Helen Kowalska was declared Blessed by Pope John Paul II.

Mr. and Mrs. Saint

If you would like to rest in peace someday,
Don't get buried in Spain.
It appears there's a problem there
With letting dead bodies be.

St. Teresa of Avila is said to have lost a hand or two because her appendages were credited with miraculous powers. The Grand Inquisitor Torquemada's tomb was ransacked by a revolutionary mob in the last century, and French forces under Napoleon desecrated the crypt of Ferdinand and Isabella's son, Juan.

Then there were the traveling royals. Queen Isabella built her tomb in Toledo, but was buried in a convent in Granada, and then moved to the royal chapel a mile away. She would have been moved again had her grandson Charles finished the cathedral in time. Instead, she remained in the chapel to be joined eventually by her husband Ferdinand, her daughter Joanna the Mad and Joanna's husband Felipe. His coffin and corpse had racked up the most mileage since Joanna had been dragging it around with her for years wherever she went.

Perhaps no one's rest was disturbed more often than that of Isidore of Madrid. Whenever drought threatened the city, his remains were taken from St. Andrew's church and paraded around town until the weather changed. Eventually he must have lost his way back from one of these meteorological sojourns because the tomb at St. Andrew's lies empty.

In an odd twist of fate, Isidore was perhaps more active dead than alive. He was a farm laborer remembered for not laboring too hard. His fellow workers complained he arrived late everyday. Their charge turned out to be true. Isidore never went to work without first going to Mass. His prayers must have been efficacious because his portion of the fields always seemed favored with the right combination of sunshine and rain. He not only turned out to be very productive, but his kindness and good humor soon won over his peers and his boss.

Isidore's saintliness was noted while he still lived, and wonderful stories grew up around him. He brought dozens of poor to a church dinner one night only to be told there wasn't enough for so many extra guests. He said Christ would provide, and indeed everything turned out fine. He fed hungry birds from sacks of grain he was supposed to take to the mill to be ground, but when he arrived at the mill, the sacks were still full. His plow team was often seen accompanied by an extra team of pure white oxen unknown to anyone in the territory.

Isidore became one of the most beloved figures in popular Spanish folklore, and is venerated with the likes of St. Ignatius Loyola and St. Francis Xavier. Unlike them, he was never far from home, nor influential in the Church, but simply known for solid goodness. His love of God, God's earth and God's creatures led the Church to consider him a true model for all who work the land. The Catholic Rural Life Conference in America honors him as its patron.

Isidore died on May 15th, 1130. A good man, he also had a good woman at his side as partner and helpmate. St. Maria de la Cabeza outlived her husband only a few years. In "Plowshares," the newsletter of the Ohio Catholic Rural Life Conference, writer Mary Kay Hummel aptly sums up Isidore's ironic place in Spanish history. Much of what she writes can also be said of Mrs. Saint:

> In an age when holiness was associated with celibacy and the monastery, Isidore was a married layman. In an age when courage and valor were associated with armies reclaiming Spain from the Moors, Isidore was a civilian. In an age when the wealthy were being awarded large tracts of land, Isidore was a poor man, a mere "hired hand" with no hope of ever owning a farm, much less an estate.

Sound bowels and sprightly eyes

I once promised some teenagers in a former parish that I would take them water skiing if only they would help me get my boat started. Several of them were mechanically minded, so they readily agreed. I forgot to mention that the boat might be hard to start since it was lying on the bottom of the lake.

They were somewhat surprised when they piled out of the car at the dock to see only the boat's flagpole sticking above water with its little plastic flag with the albatross on it. I believe only their deeply-rooted Catholic fear of the sin of "sacrilege against a sacred person" kept them from tossing me in the lake.

I told them to calm down, that we would have the boat up and running in no time. All we had to do was to lay a sturdy beam across the uprights of the dock and attach some block and tackle to it. Then, someone could dive underwater and pass a chain under the hull of the boat, and *voila!* We would raise my vessel.

I had never seen so many simultaneous expressions of stunned disbelief before. So I told them about St. Benezet.

Benezet knew nothing about engineering. He was a shepherd. And this gave him a lot of time to think about the number of people that were drowned each year as they tried to cross the nearby Rhone River in Southern France.

So he decided to build a bridge. He convinced the bishop

that God had set him to this task, and Benezet got the approval and help he needed. More experienced hands did a lot of the work, but Benezet directed the whole effort.

Then, after seven years of hard work, and just as the bridge was about to open for business, he died. His saintly demeanor, and his reputation for miracles, inspired his fellow workers to carry on however. So the work was completed around 1185.

The townspeople added a little chapel to the bridge and buried Benezet in it. There he lay for five hundred years until a flood damaged the bridge and the chapel, and washed his coffin downstream.

Folks retrieved the coffin and opened it up. They were joyously surprised when they saw that Benezet's body had not been corrupted by death. It's reported, "even the bowels were perfectly sound, and the color of the eyes lively and sprightly."

His feast is celebrated April 14th.

Thus inspired by saintly heroism, my crew turned to the task at hand. As divers with chains disappeared beneath murky waters, would-be Benezet's hoisted a heavy beam three feet in the air across the sturdy poles of the dock.

I was sitting, working on a little "Beam" of my own and a roast beef sandwich though when I heard one malcontent mumble something about wondering if a body found floating in that lake years from then might too have "lively eyes."

Godric of Finchale

I had just five friends in life and two of them were snakes

Godric of Finchale has been called a living battleground where God fought it out with the World, the Flesh and the Devil. God must have won because Godric's feast is celebrated May 21st. The battle could not have been an easy one though. When Godric was over 100 years old, a monk asked him if he could write his biography. Godric replied:

You would attempt to write the life of a bawdy rascal? Very good, here are the headings. Godric is a country clod and fat. He used to be a fornicator, adulterer and dirty hound, who practiced usury in his business dealings, and gave false measure and deceived the unwary. Now he is a hermit, but a hypocrite; a solitary, forsooth, whose head is crowded with vile thoughts; a glutton and covetous fellow who here devours and dissipates the alms of the charitable. Godric likes his ease and can often be found both day and night snoring luxuriously. He is also fond of the praises of men. Write these and worse things about Godric if you would show him to the world truly for the monster he is.

Godric was being a little hard on himself. True, he had been a peddler and perhaps not completely honest at it. True, he had been a merchant captain and maybe dabbled a bit in piracy. True, he had seen his share of wild ports and wild times.

But he had also been on pilgrimage to Rome three times and to Jerusalem twice. He may even have saved its Christian king from the Moslems when Baldwin I was in full flight. An ancient chronicle of the crusades describes the king as saving himself and his horse by jumping aboard the ship of an English pirate named Goderic who outran the Egyptian blockade.

Furthermore, Godric was always a dutiful son. When his father, mother, sister and brother had little to eat at home, he went down to the shore to look for crabs or whatever food he could find. He came across three porpoises stranded on a tidal beach — one dead, two alive. Leaving the two to be rescued by the incoming tide, he picked up the dead porpoise and headed home. The tide rose higher and higher until it was up to the young man's nose. But conscious of the hunger at home, he refused to drop dinner, and almost drowned before he got the meal safely to shore.

In the course of his adventures, Godric became impressed with the many shrines, large and small, that he visited along the way, and with the lives of the saints associated with them. Especially enamored with the story of the hermit St. Cuthbert, young Godric vowed he would be a hermit too.

When he was almost fifty years old he fulfilled his vow. Like St. Augustine once said, "Lord, give me chastity, but not yet."

Godric chose for his hermitage a snake-infested wood called Finchale in northeast England. At last he wanted to be alone with God, and for 60 years he was — if one doesn't count visiting scholars wanting insight, Benedictines, Cistercians, priests, townsfolk, the sick seeking healing, the hungry looking for food, Scottish soldiers searching for booty and Thomas Becket asking for advice.

Godric had no formal learning, but certainly a rather wide

range of experiences for a hermit. He coupled these with mystic visions and deep insight into himself and human nature in general.

Finally, he was to the wildlife of his woods what St. Francis was to the tamer hills of Assisi. He told his biographer that he had had five friends in life and two of them were snakes. His reptilian neighbors and all others mourned his passing in 1170.

The problem with this news-paper...

...is that it never runs pictures of car wrecks on the cover. In *The Shipping News*, a novel by E. Annie Proulx, a little newspaper in Newfoundland always runs pictures of car wrecks on the cover. If no car wrecks have occurred, no problem, they run old photos from their thick file of car wreck pictures.

I don't have a story of a car wreck to tell, but I do have one about a career wreck, that of St. Philip Neri. It could be called "He Might Have Worn Clown Shoes, But He Did Save the Gypsies."

Neri grew up in Florence where he was enthralled by the fiery memory of Savonarola, a reforming cleric who did a lot to renew the Church there until he was burned at the stake.

As a young man, Neri demonstrated a lot of interest in discussions about faith and morals, and it was no real surprise when he gave up a future career in his uncle's business to move to Rome to become a student of theology and philosophy.

But then, after just three years, he left school in 1538 to become a lay preacher in the streets of Rome for thirteen years.

The city certainly needed renewal. It had been sacked by the emperor's troops and racked by clerical corruption and abuse. Neri's good humor and magnetic personality attracted many young people to what he had to say about God's love and the Christian's call to holiness.

In his famous white shoes, made of cheap untanned

leather, he clopped about the streets of Rome, joking, jesting, but always challenging all to reform and renewal in their lives. One tactic was to visit seven notable churches of Rome in a pilgrimage around the city that included prayers, hymns, popular songs, and even a picnic along the way.

Eventually, friends convinced him to become a priest, and soon other clergy were gathered around him in an institute that became the Oratorian Fathers.

They lived in a community that invited the laity in every afternoon for a round of prayer, study and lively discussion. Folks listened to Neri's sermons and sang Palestrina's songs for weeks on end — something like an endless string of days of recollection.

Philip had his detractors though. Twice his work was interrupted by papal investigations into charges that ranged from his pilgrimages being drunken frolics to laymen preaching Protestantism in the Oratory's daily gatherings.

His holy career looked wrecked, but he was cleared both times, and carried on his special apostolate. Once again, he appeared to be in trouble when he joined other preachers in petitioning the pope to stop the drafting of Gypsies for forced labor, to row Christian galleys in a war against the Turks. The petition was accepted but all the signers except Neri found themselves exiled from the city.

Philip Neri joked with street children and shared flasks with friends, but he also gave sound counsel to the likes of Ignatius of Loyola and Francis de Sales. On May 26, 1595, the eighty-year-old "Christian Socrates" and "Apostle of Rome" heard confessions and saw visitors all day, and then simply told a friend, "Last of all, we must die."

MARGARET POLE

A woman for all seasons

Blessed Margaret Pole had three sons. One was executed for treason. A second testified against him. And a third got her head chopped off. When she first bore her children, her prospects certainly looked brighter than that.

She was married to the high-ranking Earl of Salisbury, a close friend of King Henry VIII, and her sons' hearts pumped the royal blood of both the Plantagenet and Tudor lines. Further, Margaret became such a close friend of Henry's wife, Catherine, that she was appointed Confirmation sponsor and governess of the royal daughter, Mary. Margaret's lofty status looked secure indeed.

Then Henry met Anne Boleyn. The encounter was no accident of course. Henry was casting about for a replacement for the queen who had not borne him a son. When the papacy would not grant him an annulment, he divorced Catherine anyway and married Anne.

The very devout Margaret could not approve, and quietly withdrew from court life to her country estates. Princess Mary was taken from her care, and the 63 year-old governess missed her mightily since she had been like a second mother to the child.

Perhaps she could have lived out her remaining years in sad peace if her gifted son Reginald had possessed less integrity or more prudence.

By 1534 the breach between Henry and the pope had become complete. The king forced through Parliament the Act of Supremacy which declared Henry head of Christianity in England, the one anointed by God "who directs the life of his Church, guards and declares its teachings, gives its bishops their jurisdiction, and corrects its people."

Some could privately scoff at the notion, but public figures like Sir Thomas More and Bishop John Fisher were eventually forced to take a stand on the issue, and lost their heads over it. Lady Margaret was silent about the Act, and her age and royal blood at first protected her from involvement.

But King Henry insisted that her son Reginald, a noted theologian and advisor to the pope, indicate yes or no did he agree to the Act. Reginald didn't say no. He said hell no, absolutely no, resoundingly no, unequivocally no. His treatise on the Defense of the Church's Unity denounced Henry's claim to lordship over the English Church.

The king was furious. Reginald had been a favorite. In an early form of government grant, Henry had even paid his tuition at Oxford. The king summoned his royal cousin home, but Reginald refused quoting the fable of the cautious animal who saw the footsteps of "those who went into the lion's den but none of any who came out."

Cardinal Pole has been criticized by some for his bravery from afar, and blamed for his mother's downfall. His defenders support his honesty and claim that precisely because of his relationship to both Henry and the pope he above all others had to oppose the king.

At any rate, Reginald's family back home was arrested, one brother testified under duress that indeed the other was disloyal and threatening rebellion. The eldest son was done away with and the family lands confiscated. Margaret was questioned for months, but even her inquisitors admired her honesty and saintliness, and told the king they could find no disloyalty to charge her with in court.

It took a special bill of Parliament to deny Margaret trial under the law. She was simply voted guilty of treason and condemned for supporting uprisings against the king.

Over 70 now, she was imprisoned in the Tower of London for two years and then, on an hour's notice, led to the executioner's axe. In happier times, someone had said that there was "no nobler nor more devout woman in all of England." The speaker was Henry VIII. Her feast is celebrated May 28th.

The blood of African martyrs

Kabaka — King
Lubiri — Palace
Praying Ones — Ugandan Christians
Page — Young Nobleman In Service to
 the King
Until He Becomes A Warrior

In 1878, Catholic missionaries from France made their way into what is now part of Uganda. Their goal was to staff an orphanage for ransomed slave children and convert them to Christianity.

But after just four years, they gave up. The kabaka wasn't friendly; the populace seemed uninterested; and the orphans appeared discontented.

Maybe it was best they left for a time, for while they were gone, Africans began to quietly convert one another. A few remembered the lessons taught and the Good News of Christ and shared these with others.

The missionaries came back in 1885 to find a growing community of believers and a new kabaka, Mwanga, who had succeeded his deceased father.

At the same time, however, many African leaders were beginning to suspect missionaries as just another weapon in European efforts to dominate them and carve up their continent.

Mwanga turned out to be one of these wary kings. When

he heard from Anglican missionaries that their bishop was on the way with even more preachers, he felt threatened. One of his Catholic officials, Joseph Mukasa, tried to convince his king that missionaries were different from colonizers. But Mwanga didn't see it that way.

He despatched some loyal soldiers who killed Bishop Harrington. Moreover, he began to doubt Joseph's loyalty.

To the king, Christians seemed out of place, with their strange god calling upon them to deviate from long established customs and traditions. In reality, they may have been obedient subjects in general, but not in areas where the king's commands or tribal practices ran afoul of their new faith.

There were a good number of praying ones right in the lubiri among the king's own pages. Joseph tried to coach them in just how to be loyal servants and good Christians at the same time. But his work turned out to be fruitless.

Instead, he became the first Catholic martyr of Uganda. Mwanga became convinced he couldn't be trusted and ordered him burned to death. The chief executioner tried to stall. He knew and respected Mukasa. But the order was confirmed. Still, the executioner spared Joseph death by fire by cutting off his head before he was placed in the flames.

Over twenty-five young pages were not so lucky the next Spring. Refusal to obey an immoral command of Mwanga may have been the final cause of their execution, but the king's displeasure with them had been growing for a long time. He had them locked away for a brief time, and then marched to Namugongo, where they were wrapped in reed mats, set on a great pyre, and burned to death on June 3rd, 1886.

A few had been pardoned at the last minute, and they are a source for most accounts of the Ugandan martyrs.

COLUMCILLE

If it's your cow, it's your calf

Most of us remember learning our ABC's by memorizing an old rhyming song. Columcille's teachers had a more nutritious approach. They printed the alphabet on a loaf of biscuit and simply fed it to their young student. Significantly, he ate half of the loaf on one side of a stream, crossed over, and finished it on the other side, an ambulatory prophecy of his future career on both sides of the Irish Sea.

A century before, young St. Patrick had been a slave. Later St. Brigid's mother had been a slave, and the young girl had often worked in her mother's place. But Columcille, the third of Ireland's great patron saints, was born to royalty, a member of the family which provided Ireland some of its high kings.

He was born in 521 in Donegal where the land lies so far west that inhabitants are known to sometimes gaze out on the Atlantic and murmur, "next parish, America." His name was Crimthain. Later he would be called Columba in Church circles. But because he liked to play around a neighborhood chapel so much, his friends dubbed him *colum cille* — dove of the Church.

As was the custom with royal sons, Columcille was sent away to be tutored by learned monks. He was a bright and popular student and sometime during his schooling he made the decision to avoid a future in clan governance and to pursue a career in the Church instead.

On a break from his studies, he and a cousin traveled

north where they met a Bishop Etchen out plowing his fields. They asked the bishop to ordain them, and with a typically Celtic sense of priority, the bishop said he would, but only after he had finished his plowing.

Columcille eventually journeyed to Derry where he founded a monastery. According to whose accounts you believe, it was the first of a hundred to three hundred more, in Ireland, Scotland and the North of England. He spent sixteen very happy years at Derry, traveling some to oversee his other monasteries in Ireland, where monks worked, prayed, studied and created some of the most beautiful manuscripts of the Scriptures the world has ever seen.

His story might have ended happily in Ireland, but at this point in the saint's life, a dark and murky tale unfolds. In the story, Abbot Columcille is visiting his friend Abbot Finnian who has just acquired a beautiful manuscript of some of the Scriptures. Columcille asks permission to make a copy but is refused. So for several nights, Columcille copies while Finnian dozes.

When Finnian awakes to the deception, he cries the ancient Gaelic version of "copyright violation" and both abbots rush off to King Dermott for judgment. In a pithy but sublime bit of jurisprudence that has echoed down the centuries, Dermott pronounces *"le gach boin a buinin"* — with every cow goes its calf — and gives the copy back to Finnian. A furious Columcille storms out. Things then get really bad.

A clansman of Columcille accidentally kills a clansman of the king in a game of hurling that gets out of hand. The clansman flees to the highborn Columcille for protection, but the king's officers brush the abbot aside and return the fugitive to swift and deadly justice. Now a furious and humiliated Columcille heads home where northern clans rise in outrage against the king. A bloody battle ensues in the lovely Sligo countryside and losses on both sides are severe.

A stricken Columcille blames himself and his temper. He says he had forsaken an earthly kingdom to serve the kingdom of God and he had ill served them both. Either as part of his own remorse or to fulfill a penance assigned by his confessor, Columcille vows to leave his beloved Ireland forever and sets out with a dozen companions on perilous journeys and exciting lives that would see the founding of the great monastery of Iona and many, many more throughout the British Isles.

Columcille's fame grew in his lifetime and inflated tremendously after his death. He became credited with prophecies that always came true, miraculous cures, and even the ability to raise the dead. But he is also remembered for an essentially Gaelic personality that was "devout, fiery, energetic, romantic, and able."

His monks are credited with bringing Christianity to pagan Scotland and with reintroducing it to England and parts of Europe where barbarian invasions had endangered it. But the Irish remember him as one of their own who did indeed return to them one day when his coffin washed ashore on his native Erin. His feast is celebrated June 8th.

STEPHEN

Don't give up the ship

I was deeply disappointed to hear that recent efforts to raise the Titanic have failed, and may even have resulted in further damage to the ship. As someone whose fiberglass speed boat has sunk a few times itself, I can sympathize with those trying to save another classic vessel.

Of course, they couldn't use the block and tackle method of stretching a beam across their dock and lowering a chain around the boat to crank it up with. The last time I used that method, someone asked me how I knew it would work.

"Simple," I said, "I've done it before with this very same boat."

"Why?" They asked.

"Because the guy at the marina sold his tow truck with the big lift on it. You see," I explained, "the first two times the boat sank, I simply called this guy named Frank and he came over with a big tow truck and just hoisted the boat right out of the water. It was the neatest thing I've ever seen, and I only had to pay him $75.00."

"But, you say, he sold the truck? Why?"

"Because, he told me, he didn't think that there would be much use for it around such a shallow lake."

"He didn't know you very well. Did he?"

"No, I guess he didn't. Now keep cranking the chain or we'll never get to go boating."

It's obvious, of course, that Frank gave up too soon. There was at least another $150.00 he could have made out of that truck. He needed some of the stuff of St. Stephen of Perm.

Stephen was adamant about one thing: he would bring Christianity to the people of the Ural Mountains, and he would respect their culture at the same time.

He had already been a Russian Orthodox monk for 13 years when he set out from Rostov to bring Christ to the Zyryan people. But he didn't want his faith to be seen as something foreign and strange.

So he translated the Scriptures and the words of the liturgy into the Zyryan language, and even invented an alphabet for them to use. Instead of imposing Russian or Greek letters on them, he adapted their own symbols and designs that he saw on their clothing and their carvings.

He did everything he could to attract them to the Faith, making public worship very dramatic and majestic in order to hold their attention. After they had become believers, he kept them close to the Church by his charity and benevolence toward all.

Would succeeding generations come to know Christ? Stephen founded schools and seminaries to see that they would, and worked hard as the first bishop of Perm to help keep their faith alive.

Stephen died in Moscow on April 26, 1396. Thanks partly to his work, Zyryan is spoken in the Urals to this day. If you go there, pronounce all your p's, but keep your b's silent. Thus one would be speaking of raising their 'oat out of the water.

Chapter III

JOHN FISHER

The man for all seasons' next door neighbor

Saint Thomas More always was famous, but he has become even better known in recent years due to the film "A Man for All Seasons." Who hasn't cried at Paul Scofield's emotional farewell scene with More's wife and daughter? Some of us were equally moved by the great banquet scenes in Henry VIII's castles. Imagine people eating so many different kinds of birds at one meal.

I once drove out from London to not see Henry's palace at Hampton Court. It was during the same trip that I went down to Dover to not see the white cliffs, and over to Windsor to not see the changing of the guard. The fog was so thick that week that it gave whole new meaning to the tourist phrase "off-season."

I did however get to see the Great Kitchen at Hampton Court where some of Henry's banquets were prepared and from which More himself was doubtlessly fed. It's possible that sitting next to More at one of these meals would have been John Fisher, Bishop of Rochester. He eventually came to live on the same block as More; the same cell block that is.

Fisher was born in Yorkshire, educated at Cambridge and became both Bishop of Rochester and chancellor of his alma mater in 1504. His reputation for both saintliness and intelligence grew with every sermon he preached and each new book he wrote. Perhaps it was this very fame that helped begin his long slide toward his doom.

Henry VIII, as is well known, wanted to divorce Catherine of Aragon so that he could marry Anne Boleyn. He sent his chancellor Cardinal Wolsey to the learned and respected Fisher to get an opinion on a way to get the marriage annulled.

What Henry wanted Fisher to say was that the pope had erred in giving him a dispensation to marry Catherine in the first place since Church law then forbade a person marrying his brother's widow. Fisher thought about it for three months and said, "No."

Henry should have guessed it. True, Fisher was a friend. He had been Henry's grandmother's confessor, had preached at Henry's father's funeral, and had even tutored and guided the young Henry at Cambridge.

But Fisher had also vehemently defended the Roman Catholic Church and the papacy from attacks by the Lutherans and other "heretics," even to the point of condemning a Protestant Bible smuggler to death at the stake. He wasn't about to agree that the pope had exceeded his powers in giving Henry a marriage dispensation.

When Henry had the House of Commons vote himself head of the Church in England, More quietly resigned from Henry's government. But as a bishop of his rank, Fisher sat in the House of Lords where he led the opposition to the steps the Commons was taking to help Henry have his way.

Grandma's confessor was becoming quite a problem. First Henry had him tried and fined 300 pounds for not reporting to Henry on the crazed revelations of Elizabeth Barton, the Nun of Kent. In a prophecy that publicly embarrassed the government, the mystic had foretold Henry's quick demise if he married Anne. With Henry still around and happily married a year later, her prophecy lost its punch and Elizabeth lost her life.

Fisher returned to the quiet of Rochester but only for a few years. Famous men like him and More could not be left alone when it came to recognizing Henry's place as head of the Church of England.

They were arrested and condemned under the Act of Treason, a new law to punish anyone who did not recognize all the formal titles Henry had amassed for himself. In prison for a year, Fisher was not allowed any books to read. So instead he wrote three of his own.

On June 22nd, 1535, he was beheaded. On the 23rd, his head was parboiled and placed on a spike on London Bridge for two weeks until it was thrown into the river to make room for More's.

JOSEPH CAFASSO

Hanged saints and boys' clubs

Brigands, thieves, murderers, treasonous soldiers, all condemned to die by the courts of Turin in Northern Italy, and all going to their deaths in the company of a small and bent confessor who called them his "hanged saints."

Father Joseph Cafasso had to struggle to make time for his prison ministry. After all, he was already rector of an institute for the pastoral training of young priests, and director of a popular shrine up in the hills.

But he saw his work with convicts and the condemned as part of his larger vocation to reconcile, to encourage, to console and to enlighten all about the length and breadth of the mercy of God. The only ones he grew impatient with were fellow priests who were too unkind in the confessional or too strict with the erring.

As rector of the institute, he did indeed influence a whole generation of future pastors and preachers with his kind, good nature, his demanding discipline and his lectures in moral theology; but he was loved too by the faithful because of his love for them and for their loved ones in jail. A contemporary writes that once Father Cafasso was so caught up in one of his lengthy visits to a prison that he lost all track of time so that...

> ...the gates of the prison had already been locked and bolted, and he faced the prospect of spending the

night with the inmates. But then came the guards for their inspection, carrying lanterns at the end of long iron rods, and armed with rifles, pistols and swords. While they were checking the walls and walks for possible escape attempts, they noticed a stranger among the convicts. "Who goes there," they shouted and, without waiting for an answer, they surrounded Father Cafasso. "What are you doing here?" they asked. "Who are you? Stand still; don't move! Tell us who you are!"

"I am Father Cafasso." "Father Cafasso! What? At this hour? Why didn't you leave earlier? We can't get you out of the prison without making a report to the warden."

"I don't mind. Make your report to whom you like. But you had better think it over, because you should have been here sooner, before nightfall, to check that all visitors had left the prison precincts. That was your duty, and you are at fault."

They were silent for a moment, and then begged Father Cafasso to keep the matter quiet. They not only opened the gates for him, but to gain his good-will, they even accompanied him home.

Who was the admirer that passed on the tale of Cafasso's "jailbreak"? It was the future St. John Bosco, at that time a young priest at Cafasso's institute. Bosco also writes that in the seminary he learned dogma, but that, with Cafasso, he learned how to be a priest. It was after he had accompanied Cafasso on his prison rounds that Bosco formed his idea of helping the young avoid trouble by offering better alternatives. Further, he says of Cafasso, "If I have been able to do any good, I owe it to this worthy priest in whose hands I placed every decision I made, all my study and every activity of my life."

St. Joseph Cafasso died June 23rd, 1860, just about a year after his young pupil John Bosco had begun his society known today as the Salesians. They run a youth center here in Columbus on South Sixth Street. I went there as a kid and have avoided jail to this day — well, at least in this country. There was that time after a roasted goose with extra rum sauce at Dyker and Thuys in Amsterdam.

Oliver Plunkett

MacMoyer showed up drunk, and said Murphy could not be found

One thing the English excelled at was making Irish martyrs. Henry VIII, for example, when he was finished with English Catholics like Thomas More and John Fisher, turned on Ireland next, confiscating monasteries, seizing lands, and insisting that the Irish recognize him not only as king but as head of the Church too. Those who opposed him risked their lives.

Subsequent English monarchs followed policies toward Ireland that ranged from grudging tolerance of Catholics to outright persecution of all things "papist." None of them however is remembered with such dread among the Irish as Oliver Cromwell, the Puritan general who held Catholicism and the monarchy in equal disdain.

Among the Irish, "the curse of Cromwell on you" is still a much feared hex. After defeating the army of King Charles I and lopping off that unfortunate's head, Cromwell came to Ireland to put down a rebellion against English rule.

Wherever he went, towns that submitted were spared, but those that resisted were put to the torch with unarmed citizens often executed along with the defeated rebel garrisons. At Drogheda, some townspeople climbed into a church steeple only to see Cromwell's men piling the pews under the steeple and setting them ablaze. One observant fugitive was heard to cry, "God damn me, God confound me. I burn. I burn."

While Oliver Cromwell was leveling monasteries in Ireland, another Oliver was teaching in them in Italy. Oliver Plunkett had left his native Dublin in 1645 to study under the Jesuits in Rome. He was ordained there in 1654, but couldn't go home while the other Oliver was there. So he became a noted instructor in theology and philosophy instead.

Even after Cromwell's death, the persecution of Catholicism in Ireland continued. Some bishops were executed, some were exiled and some went into hiding. In 1670, Armagh, the most ancient and important see in Ireland was vacant. Knowing Plunkett's sound intellect and character firsthand, the pope asked Oliver to become archbishop of the original see of St. Patrick himself.

I'm not sure it was a promotion. Plunkett arrived in his new diocese wearing a wig and carrying a sword and two pistols. He went by the name of Captain Brown to avoid the priesthunters he knew were after him. He slept where he could and ate what his friends could spare. Only after a year of constantly moving about, and ordaining priests in secret, was he able to come out of hiding. A brief period of religious tolerance had returned to Ireland.

Plunkett founded schools, convoked gatherings of bishops, and confirmed over 50,000 souls in less than four years. But the archbishop had to walk a delicate tightrope. English authorities expected him to help keep the peace. Irish patriots wanted a nationalist leader. Plunkett merely wanted to unite, reorganize and restore Catholicism in Ireland.

He might have been successful in his balancing act had it not been for Reverend Titus Oates and Lord Shaftesbury over in England. Oates possibly had it in for Catholics, having been expelled twice from Jesuit seminaries. From his Anglican pulpit, he claimed sure knowledge of a Popish Plot brewing that would see the massacre of Protestants, the landing of the French at Dover, and the Jesuits taking over command of the army and the navy.

The hysteria whipped up by Oates helped the parliamentary leader Lord Shaftesbury block the new king's efforts at religious tolerance in his realm. Instead, English Catholics were once again tried and executed for disloyalty, and the furor then spread to Ireland where Archbishop Plunkett was arrested for treason.

At his first trial in Ireland, two ex-priests were supposed to supply evidence of his guilt, but one showed up drunk and said he couldn't find the other. Plunkett was acquitted but Shaftesbury had him arrested again and brought to trial in London before a biased judge and jury.

Nine witnesses charged him with everything from secretly collecting arms to choosing a landing site for a French invasion. The jury deliberated fifteen minutes before pronouncing him guilty. Blessed Oliver Plunkett was hanged July 1st, 1681. His entrails were burned and his head chopped off for good measure.

In *Irish Saints*, Robert Reilly tells of a certain Hugh Duffy, one of the prosecution witnesses, showing up in Armagh 40 years later to seek forgiveness. In the bishop's house, he was led to a shrine in the corner. The cabinet doors were opened and there on a platter Duffy saw the head of Oliver Plunkett. He fainted.

You can see the head too in the same Drogheda the other Oliver sacked, in the parish church of St. Peter's. Or you may simply prefer the view of the River Boyne out the windows of the Buttergate Inn. Try the seafood crepes.

JAN HUS

The council was Constance, but the emperor not constant

A spokesman for the Roman Catholic Church in the Czech Republic recently reported that the case of Jan Hus is being reconsidered, but that his "rehabilitation" is unlikely for the time being.

Should the 15th century Hus be rehabilitated, it's even more unlikely that his grave could become a shrine for pilgrims to visit. For the Church not only burned him at the stake, but it burned his bones too, over and over, so that nothing of Hus would remain for his friends to cart off and revere.

What was the issue? It depends on who you ask. Followers of Hus point out that he was a true reformer, desiring to purify the Church by returning it to Gospel values of poverty, simplicity, and detachment. Like Hus, they would emphasize the primacy of Scripture as the Christian's only sure guide.

Opponents claim Hus denied the proper place of the papacy and the Church itself in leading souls to salvation, and that he taught heresy concerning the Sacraments.

The Council of Constance sided with the latter. The Council had met to heal the Great Schism in which several different popes were claiming to be the true successor to St. Peter.

The German Emperor Sigusmund, who forced the Council to be called in the first place, thought it should also address the problem of disunity among Christians in Bohemia. Followers of Hus, the rector of the University of Prague, were agitating for greater Czech independence in spiritual affairs and less interference from foreign churchmen.

Sigusmund thought Hus should come to address the Council and attempt a reconciliation between the "Hussites" and the wider Church. And the emperor promised the priest safe conduct to and from the Council in Germany.

But when Hus was questioned and found guilty of heresy, the emperor reneged and withdrew the safe conduct. Repeatedly, Hus was urged to recant. It seems no one wanted an execution, not the cardinals struggling for Church unity after years of discord, not Sigusmund who would look villainous to his Czech subjects, and certainly not Hus' friends who pleaded with him to save himself.

Hus would not be budged. When forty-five articles titled heresies were presented to him, he rejected most of them as not being what he taught. Some, though, he would not deny unless they could be proved wrong by arguments from the Bible alone. Others he claimed were erroneous presentations of his opinions made by false witnesses in the first place.

Jan Hus was found guilty by the Council and turned over to the secular authorities who burned him and his books on July 6, 1415. Czechs waged a rebellion against the German-dominated empire for years, with religious disagreements as a prime motivation. Jan Hus became a national hero and symbol of Czech pride.

Visiting Prague in 1990, Pope John Paul II praised Hus' "personal integrity of life." But even the dean of the University of Prague's faculty of Protestant theology admits a change in Constance's verdict is unlikely.

I bid two pastries and a firecracker

The best Fourth of July I ever had was July 3rd about ten years ago. Some friends and I had boarded a Canadian sternwheeler for a leisurely cruise down the St. Lawrence. The captain welcomed us aboard and remarked that we seemed younger than his usual passenger list of retirees. We thanked him and didn't mention that we merely needed his boat as a floating card table for a game of bid euchre that had been going on for years on planes, trains and auto-ferries on both sides of the iron curtain.

The boat wasn't large, but it was comfortable, and the food was very good. It was nice not to have any language barriers to surmount too. I'm sure the bartender was French Canadian but when one of our group asked him if he had any Pernod, and started to spell out P-E-R..., the barman curtly responded, "Yes, I know how to spell it, and, no, we don't have it."

On the first day, our captain kept the card table steady on its stately progress toward Montreal. But our game that night was suddenly interrupted by bright flashes and loud explosions. It seems the Canadians on the north shore were continuing their weekend celebration of Canada Day.

Then, when the boat docked at a small village for refueling, the band in the lounge started playing music that Lawrence Welk's parents may have once danced to. It was impossible to concentrate with all the noise. So we jumped ship for a walk though town, and, of all things, ended up at a parish festival.

It was fun. No one complained to *me* when the toilet paper ran out in the ladies room, or when the eight-year-olds started betting at the craps tables. Before long, we found out the festival was in honor of St. Elizabeth of Portugal on the eve of her feast day, July 4th. That explained the delicious *arrufadas* they were selling at the dessert table.

Elizabeth was the daughter of King Peter of Aragon. Her great aunt was the more famous St. Elizabeth of Hungary (although she wasn't called that yet). Young Elizabeth was beautiful, talented and bright. And she had already earned a reputation for kindness and generosity to the poor. So it was considered a great day for Portugal when she was married to their young king Denis.

The marriage did seem blessed. The couple was in love, and they had two sons. But Denis proved unworthy of such a mate. He drank and partied too much. He ran around on her. And he caused public scandal and embarrassment.

Elizabeth kept her disappointment to herself, prayed for her husband, and redoubled her works of mercy at hospitals and asylums. One story has it that when she went to help wash a patient, the woman hid one of her feet from the queen because it was horrid-looking with a bleeding sore. Elizabeth not only washed the foot, she bent and kissed it. The sore healed.

Elizabeth was then called to be a healer on a broader stage. Denis eventually came to a change of heart and a change of behavior. He begged her forgiveness, and she became the peacemaker of the kingdom. When their son Alphonse led a rebellion against the king, she rode out alone between the battle lines, and successfully entreated her son to reconcile with his father.

Years later, as a widow, she left the quiet of her small house near her beloved Poor Clares when war seemed immi-

nent between Portugal and Castile. Again, her personal inter-
vention and exalted reputation for goodness brought peace.

Unfortunately, the journey wore her out. She caught fever and died in 1336. She is buried at Santa Clara Convent in
Coimbra along the River Mondego. The curved pastry *arrufada*
gets its name from that winding waterway.

The St. Lawrence doesn't wind too much though. So on
the Fourth we were able to resume our game in peace — that
is until nightfall when the noise started up all over again from
the U.S. side.

Bishops Grassi and Fogalla

Where's Moses when you really need him?

In the last century, Europeans brought the Chinese: Christian missionaries, foreign aggression, and opium addiction. The Chinese might then be forgiven for confusing the fervor of the Fathers with the interference of Occidental diplomats and traders.

Resentment of all three boiled over in the summer of 1900. The government of the dowager Ch'ing empress secretly supported mob violence against Europeans and Chinese Christians in northern China that year.

The spearhead of the anti-foreign movement were called the Boxers by Europeans, and were the outgrowth of a secret, revolutionary society known as the Righteous and Harmonious Fists.

The empress sought to channel the energies of the society against increasingly blatant foreign interference in Chinese policy, thus the misnomer Boxer Rebellion.

Many Americans are familiar with this attack on Europeans in June of 1900 because of the film "55 Days at Peking" in which Charlton Heston (aka Moses, Ben Hur, Michelangelo) and other stars like David Niven hold off the besiegers until rescue arrives.

There were no Oscar nominees in far away Taiyuanfu when the Boxers came for the Europeans and their converts. Rumors run faster than mobs though. So when the Boxers arrived on July 9th, Bishop Grassi had already closed the school and sent home all but five seminarians.

That left Grassi his assistant, Bishop Fogalla, some Franciscan priests and Sisters, and about ten adult Chinese Catholics in addition to the students. All had been confined by a Chinese official to a place known as the Inn of Heavenly Peace.

Boxer militia first killed the Protestants gathered in a separate wing of the building, and then broke in upon the Catholics. Bishop Grassi was the first to fall beneath their swords and axes, and then the others. The Chinese Catholics were offered their lives if they foreswore their religion, but reportedly none did.

Other Christians died for their faith in spots scattered around the north, but it appears Chinese officials further south suppressed Boxer uprisings there.

Meanwhile, back in Peking, an international army captured the city on August 14th, looted it, and chased the empress and her court out of town. Humiliated underlings were left to make a new treaty with the "foreign devils." A semblance of peace was restored as the imperial Chinese government continued in its decline until 1912 when the last emperor abdicated. But that's a whole other movie in which Mr. Chips plays a leading role.

> He would
> have rolled
> over in his
> grave had
> he ever got
> there

"Keep cool. Don't lose your head," is sound advice. It's good counsel for basketball teams blowing a lead, for friends letting an argument get out of hand, and for parents tempted to lash out at their children. But it would probably not have helped the Sixteen Carmelites of Compiegne. Despite their best efforts at self control, they lost their heads in 1794 — on the guillotine.

What were their crimes? They were convicted of insidious things like praying the psalms out loud, wearing religious habits, and practicing poverty, chastity and obedience together. Worse, they had gone back on the Oath.

More than a few Frenchmen (and Frenchwomen) lost their heads over the Oath. In the early months of the French Revolution, the Church was divided in its support of democratic movements. The princely bishops of the land saw themselves allied with the king and the Old Order. But many of the lower clergy supported the Revolution and were instrumental in its initial triumphs. They sought both political and religious reforms.

In 1789, the new National Assembly voted to do away with many of the nobility's and the Church's special rights and privileges. The French were to be united as one people in liberty, equality and fraternity. Instead of churchmen being supported by a special tithe they exacted from the people, they would become employees of the State.

As more radical parties gained power in the National Assembly, it went even further. It dissolved most religious Orders, especially those not connected with practical services like nursing or caring for orphans. The new Republic may not have needed the round-the-clock prayers of the cloistered Orders, but it certainly wanted their lands to sell off.

Soon laws were passed that would have pastors and bishops elected by the people, and dioceses in France all realigned to coincide with government departments.

Obedience to the changes was spotty, especially in the countryside. So the Assembly next required that all clergy swear an Oath to uphold the new laws, the Constitution, and the actions of the National Assembly both past and future.

Then the real confusion began. Many clergy sincerely took the Oath, many took it with their fingers crossed behind their backs, many refused to take the Oath at all, and many in the countryside weren't even asked to if they and the local bureaucrats were friends.

France for a time had two Catholic Churches, an official one and an unofficial one preferred by many of the people. The buildings were all turned over to the government clergy, but the other clergy could celebrate Mass in homes and barns and the like.

For a time, it appeared confusion would be the worst consequence of the arrangement. But after awhile things got ugly. Funerals for example could be celebrated at the church by the new clergy or at the cemetery by the old clergy. One poor soul whose family disagreed with one another was being carried directly to the cemetery by some of his kin when his coffin was overtaken by other relatives. In the ensuing brawl the deceased changed hands three times until the coffin was dropped and he rolled out onto the ground to be ignored by the combatants who were still going at one another.

On the national level, the Revolution was becoming radicalized as fears of foreign invasion grew. More and more people became suspected of being counter-revolutionaries and subversives. More and more were required to take the Oath including sixteen cloistered Carmelite sisters in Compiegne. More and more went to the guillotine.

Clergy and religious were among those killed, imprisoned or in exile. Some courageously went underground to continue to serve the flock. At first, the sixteen Carmelites were to take the Oath, turn over their convent and split into four households. But in June, they were arrested, taken to Paris, and thrown in prison.

Since they saw their Oath had done them no good, they renounced it. They put their habits back on, and started up their cloistered life right there in the infamous Conciergerie down the hall from Marie Antoinette's cell.

On July 17th, they were loaded into carts. Since it was a long ride to the guillotine, they had time to sing some of their favorites: *Miserere*, *Salve Regina*, and *Te Deum*. They were still singing as they mounted the steps to their execution. Each in turn blessed the next to go, and the prioress blessed herself last. They ranged in age from under thirty to almost eighty.

You can see their prison today along the River Seine on the Ile de la Cité. Le Trappiste Café across the river serves great mussels, and you can sample 180 different kinds of beer. Not all at once of course.

Bruised bathers and screaming demons

I just stopped to look at a "giant" water-slide here in Ohio along the Mohican River. The slide had four different chutes that folks could fly down to splash into a shallow pool at the end.

I was trying to figure out if one of the water routes was harder than the other when a kid walked up to me and asked if I was the health inspector. I was the only one in long pants and a dress shirt. So I must have looked official. . . .

I told him, no, I was not from the health department, that I was only the "Slide Inspector." He thought about that for a moment and then asked me if I would like to know something about slide #2. I told him, "Sure." He confided in me that half way down that chute, a vicious curve slams people into the side.

I said, "Does it cut people?" He said, "No." No one he'd seen was bleeding. I said, "Well, if no one gets cut, we can't do anything about it." He said, "Well, what if they get bruised?"

I told him bruises don't count, that there has to be blood for me to get involved. He shook his head in disgust and walked away, thoroughly disappointed in the power of authority to protect the innocent.

Too bad he never knew St. Germanus of Auxerre. Germanus was a noble Roman from the province of Gaul, a lawyer, magistrate, and respected family man, just the kind of person people insisted on for bishop. And he was a great help to those threatened with harm.

Once, an imperial tax collector stopped on his rounds to visit the bishop and left without his bag of government gold. When he found his mistake, he rushed back to the holy man's house only to find the bag not there. He begged the bishop's help since execution was in store if he couldn't restore the funds. Germanus immediately suspected a certain sinner known to be possessed by evil demons, and who, for some unexplained reason, hung around the chancery a lot. Some things never change.

When questioned, the demoniac denied doing the dirty deed. But later at Mass, Germanus prayed explicitly for him, and the poor soul rose screaming into the air shouting that he was guilty. The man than collapsed, freed from possession, and told where the gold was hidden. The tax collector was saved.

A young priest too was on a long journey with the bishop. The two of them could find only a haunted cottage to sleep in on a dark and fearsome night. The holy Germanus snored soundly, but the frightened priest stayed awake at prayer until, sure enough, a spectral figure appeared and the cleric yelled in terror.

This wakened Germanus who right away insisted that the ghost tell him who he was. The shadowy form explained that he was a dead criminal, left unburied to bother the living even in death. The bishop took pity and told the ghost to lead him to his corpse.

The ghost then produced a torch, since it was pitch black outside, and led the bishop to an overgrown garden where not one but two skeletons lay, shackled together — the ghost and his sidekick. Germanus went back to bed.

The next day, however, he returned with some villagers who cleared away the brush, broke off the shackles, and dug two graves. Germanus gave the deceased a Christian burial, and the cottage was haunted no more.

Finally, there was the time when Germanus saved two friends from harm, using the stature of his office and the power of his prayer to scare off whole invasions of Saxons and Picts threatening the Christian Britons he was visiting at the time. His feast is on July 26.

> **Basques will bet on anything that has a number on it and moves**

People commenced to come running. A drunk slipped and fell. Two policemen grabbed him and rushed him over the fence. The bulls were going fast and gaining on the crowd. Another drunk started out from the fence with a blouse in his hands. He wanted to do capework with the bulls. The two policemen tore out and collared him. One hit him with a club, and they dragged him against the fence and stood flattened out against the fence as the last of the crowd and the bulls went by. With its annual "Running of the Bulls," Pamplona was a place of dramatic change for Hemingway's young characters in *The Sun Also Rises*. So it was too in 1521 for Inigo Lopez.

Pamplona was one target of a French invasion attempting to seize the Province of Navarre from Spain. Many citizens of the town thought this change in government a great idea and so surrendered right away.

But a young knight known for his drinking, brawling and wenching as well as for his courage, ambition and bad temper, convinced the Spanish forces to retreat to the town's citadel where he assured them they could hold out. He was wrong — just about dead wrong.

The French began bombarding, and the defenders responded with their nineteen cannons. The fight lasted over six hours until the French breached the walls and poured in. Inigo kept up the fight until he was struck by a ball that shattered his right leg and wounded his left. The French let him be carried in a litter to his ancestral home to die among his fellow Basques.

For a long time it looked like he might do just that. If his wounds couldn't kill him, his vanity almost did. He insisted that his doctors operate three different times until his right leg not only worked well but looked pretty too.

Bored in bed recovering, he asked for some of the romantic tales he liked to read, but his sister's castle contained only two books, and with the French army roaming the countryside a run to the library was out of the question.

So Inigo, or Ignatius, from the Basque province of Loyola settled down to read the *Life of Christ* and the *Lives of the Saints*. The rest is Jesuit history.

Ignatius experienced some kind of conversion that, with the help of his horse, changed him forever. When he felt well enough to travel, he donned his knightly finery and set off on pilgrimage to a shrine of Mary at Montserrat. On the way, he got into a religious discussion with a Moslem who admired Jesus and who respected Mary, but who doubted her chastity in her later years.

The enraged Ignatius went for his dagger. The alarmed Moor spurred his horse down the road. The hot tempered knight knew he should pursue and wreak vengeance for the insult to Our Lady, but the novice mystic hesitated. Ignatius dropped the reins and decided to go in whatever direction his mount led; on to Montserrat, or after the Moor. He ended up at the shrine.

Ignatius struggled a great deal with guilt, with pride, with impatience to grow closer to God. The fruit of his struggle was his own maturing in faith and the writing of his *Spiritual Exercises*. The *Exercises* describe step by step instructions and meditations to help the reader move through control of self to greater union with God. Because he had to combat scrupulosity in his own development, he is offered as a patron for the scrupulous today. Biographer Rosemary Rogers thinks this is only right since, "Although throughout their history the Jesuits have been accused of many faults, having scruples has never been one of them."

The beginning of his Society of Jesus came only after years of study, pilgrimage, reflection and discussion among a small band of very bright and dedicated young men whom Ignatius gathered around himself. He resolved that if they couldn't establish themselves in the Holy Land they would go to Rome and put their destiny in the hands of the pope.

It was a terrific wager, but the Basques are notorious gamblers, and anyway, it had worked with the horse. Why not try it with a pope? From 1541 on, the first Jesuits would go on to attract others to their Order, to renounce all rank, to live under strict obedience to the pope and their superior, to combat error with scholarship, and to reform the Church from within.

Ignatius's achievements and contributions to the Church were recognized while he still lived, and princes and prelates alike mourned his passing in 1556. His feast is celebrated July 31.

DOMINIC DE GUZMAN

> # He walked over 3,000 miles

When confronted with a mechanical problem at the parish years ago, I remembered the example of the early astronauts on the moon.

A zillion dollar television camera refused to send shots back to earth. So Ground Control was getting increasingly impatient and frustrated when suddenly a picture clear as can be appeared on screens all across America.

A happy earthling asked the "Man On The Moon" how he had fixed the sensitive equipment. He responded, "I hit it with a hammer."

I figured what works with cameras can work with stuck rollers on a Xerox machine. I banged away, and *voila!* the rollers rolled. Unfortunately, so did the glass at the top of the machine, right onto the hard floor.

I guess hitting things to make them behave only works some of the time. It works often enough that we are frequently tempted to apply the same principle to people.

The Church used to do this some in the Middle Ages. When heretics in Southern France refused to see the light, and even murdered the papal legate sent to their territory, Pope Innocent III proclaimed a crusade against them. They fought back.

The Albigenses, as the heretics were called, had the support of much of the armed nobility of Southern France, who were also defending their territories and political positions against crusading nobles from the North of France. With such a balance of power in place, the war waged on and on.

Enter Domingo de Guzman.

This young nobleman from Castile had become a priest attached to the cathedral at Osma, but his great wish was to go far from home to bring Christ to pagans. On a journey to Rome to get the pope's approval for a special mission to Russia, he passed through Southern France.

There, he was impressed by the very austere and holy lives of many of the heretics, even though he decried their denial of the power of the Church's Sacraments. When the pope turned down his idea to go to Russia, Domingo found himself preaching among the Albigenses instead.

It was there that he decided that he and his fellow preachers of orthodox beliefs had to imitate the simplicity and holiness of the heretic clergy if they were going to win the common people back to the Church.

He lived in poverty, traveled the roads barefoot and insisted that his helpers do the same. Eventually, he was joined by more and more determined assistants, who were formed into the Order of Preachers, or Dominicans.

After meeting with solid success in France, Dominic set up headquarters in Rome from where he saw his Order of Preachers expand into England, Spain, Scandinavia, Poland and the Holy Land by the time he died on August 8, 1221.

He tried to visit many of his Dominicans personally, once walking from Rome to Spain and back by way of Paris, thus proving he was a much better preacher than geographer.

MAXIMILIAN KOLBE

His middle name was Mary

In October of 1982, Pope John Paul II canonized Maximilian Kolbe, a Polish priest martyred at Auschwitz on August 14, 1941. Various dignitaries attended the ceremony.

But perhaps the most significant person present was one Franciazek Gajowniczek. It was by the grace of God and Father Kolbe that this former Polish army sergeant had survived World War II.

Kolbe and the sergeant were held at the infamous concentration camp because Nazi policy called for control and annihilation of any force that could oppose its rule. The sergeant's threat to Nazi domination was obvious, but Kolbe's challenge was even more important.

He had waged war for the control of people's souls.

Born near Lodz in 1894, Kolbe joined the Franciscans as a teenager and went on to study in Rome. From ordination on, an overriding passion dominated his priesthood: to encourage and publicize devotion to Mary.

He formed a sodality, or Marian association, of friars that soon numbered in the hundreds, and distributed vast amounts of religious literature at home and abroad. He founded publishing centers as far away as Japan, and spread information about Christianity and Mary through countless supplies of little leaflets and tracts.

So when the German army occupied Poland at the beginning of the war, the Gestapo recognized Kolbe as a force to be reckoned with. He was arrested temporarily in 1939, and for good in 1941, charged with aiding Jews and the Polish resistance. Kolbe's true Marian devotion of course included all persons Mary's son had died for.

Like many brave souls of all faiths in the camps, Kolbe was a great comfort and source of kind goodness to those around him. But to none more so than Sergeant Gajowniczek.

In the summer of 1941, a prisoner escaped from the camp. The usual punishment was for ten others to die by starvation. Commandant Colonel Fritsch went down the line of inmates forced to stand at attention. Nine were chosen by number to be locked in the cellar of one of the barracks until they rotted away.

Then the colonel came to the Polish sergeant, a married man with a family. The sergeant was condemned to join the others, and muttered something about how he would miss his wife Helen and his two children.

Then Father Kolbe stepped forward. The sergeant recalls that Maximilian had a strange smile on his face as he confronted Colonel Fritsch. He could not understand everything that was said, but reports Fritsch saying, "Here's a crazy priest," and "All right."

Kolbe had volunteered to take the soldier's place.

It took days for the starving to die, and Kolbe, along with a few others, was eventually injected with poison when the cellar was needed for other things.

The martyr's birth name was Raymond, but he professed his vows as Maximilian Mary Kolbe.

> ## "The king of France won't give you his purse"

When Cardinal Richelieu wasn't occupied chasing the Three Musketeers, he was busy jailing Jansenists.

The Jansenists, named after Cornelius Jansen, the deceased bishop of Ypres, were Catholic reformers who stressed man's fallen nature so much that they believed only a few human beings could possibly be saved. You could tell who these few were because they would be the ones who hardly ever went to Confession or received Holy Communion!

You see, Jansenists viewed the two sacraments as so sacred that they felt Confession should be sought only when a person was perfectly contrite, and Communion should be received only a few times in a lifetime. This attitude was just the opposite of the frequent Confession and Communion the Council of Trent had encouraged, and which the new Jesuits were pushing everywhere.

Jansenism caused serious divisions in the French Church, and thus Richelieu's concern. One religious Order he had suspected of Jansenist tendencies was the Oratorian Fathers. And their house in the town of Samaur was still especially rigorous. So you can imagine the Oratorian priests' distaste there when Joan Delanoue started coming to daily Communion.

Joan Delanoue of all people! Wasn't she the spinster shopkeeper who stayed open Sundays to sell religious goods of all

things? Wasn't she the one who shopped for dinner right before she ate so she could tell passing beggars that she had no
food in the house to give them? Wasn't she the one who rented
a spare room to a strange old widow named Frances who
roamed from shrine to shrine murmuring "divine revelations"
that God had told her to share?

Yes, this daily communicant was that Joan who scandal-
ized villagers (and enraged competitors) by violating the Lord's
Day week after week. But she wasn't really the same Joan. She
had changed.

No one could understand most of the murmurings of the
old woman who lived with Joan, including Joan. But Joan eventually got the impression that the very devout Frances was perhaps sent to her as an agent of change.

Joan had inherited the shop when her mother died, and
the business of business was her whole life. She had gone to
church and practiced her Catholicism but only in a routine and
surface way.

But after Joan felt called to renewal, she spent a whole
Lent going from church to church to hear different preachers
and perhaps discover God's will for her life. Gradually she saw
herself called to a new business — taking care of Christ's most
helpless.

But how was she to begin? Finally Frances said something
that actually made sense, at least in a way. She told Joan, "He
(her name for God) told me that you are to go to Saint Florent
and look after six poor children in a stable there."

Joan found the children all right, and brought them home
with her. From then on, her prayer life and her good works
grew together and enriched each other. Soon she was caring
for a dozen orphans, then two dozen, then three. Instead of
hoarding money, she begged contributions for her charges
everywhere.

She gathered other women to her work, and on the feast of St. Anne, they put on religious habits and called themselves the Sisters of St. Anne of Providence.

Her orphanage kept outgrowing rented houses, stables and even caves, until wealthy benefactors heard of her work and helped her build Three Angels House that could hold 300 orphans and elderly poor.

Her Sisters grew in number and established more services for the needy all around France. Blessed Joan Delanoue worked on till age 70, dying August 17th, 1736.

She had given her life to social services long before the French government saw such things as its responsibility. Like Frances once told her in another brief moment of clarity, "The king of France won't give you his purse; but the King of kings will always keep His open for you."

BERNARD

The St. Bernard without a flask

I have a great recipe for lamb. Cut up pieces of lamb meat and throw them in a deep roasting pan. Pour in two cups each of sweet vermouth, chicken broth, and V-8 Juice. Then toss in all kinds of things like garlic cloves, onions, chopped carrots and celery. Cook it all for three hours at 325, adding cooked great northern beans toward the end to thicken things up.

It doesn't work with quail.

Having had great success with a hoofed animal, I tried the above with winged creatures. It was the noisiest dinner I ever had. The quail had all fallen off their bones and disappeared. But the bones hadn't.

First the person on my left would start hacking and coughing, and I would have to pause to start slapping him on the back; then the one on my right would break into a choking fit, and I had to stop my eating again to rescue him.

Needless to say, I could do nothing for those across from me who had to grab for what remained of the vermouth to try to wash the blue color from their faces.

The broth was wonderful though. In that sense, the quail had done its job. This is precisely what Bernard of Clairvaux did for the Church of his age. He divested himself of everything, and submerged himself entirely into the life of Christ and Christ's people, enriching, flavoring, enlivening the whole Body.

Bernard's family could afford a good education for their son, and he studied the literary classics. But when his mother died, he decided upon a life of renunciation and simplicity.

He went to the Benedictine monastery of Citeaux, from which the Cistercians get their name, and entered upon a life of prayer, reflection, and mystical union with God. He would have been happy just with that, divesting himself of all else. But his writings, sermons, and keen intellect brought him to the attention of the wider Church.

The Cistercians sent him to run a monastery at Clairvaux, but popes, rulers, universities and theologians constantly called upon him to journey away to settle disputes, preach crusades, solve theological dilemmas and even end pogroms against the Jews.

He could best heretics in debate, lecture pontiffs to their face, and denounce sin in all its guises. But he could also heal hatreds, reconcile the guilty, and calm panics. He may have been the most influential man of his age, his judgment and opinion were valued that much.

> But Bernard is timeless too.
> Whence arises the love of God?
> From God.
> And what is the measure of this love?
> To love without measure.

Bernard Tolomei

> Just because you're a saint doesn't mean you're not crazy

In 1347, Italian merchant ships arrived home from Asia Minor bringing silks, spices and tales of the infidel East. They also brought some unwelcome stowaways — big, black Asian rats, fattened by their leisurely cruise in the grain holds and swarming with fleas infected with bubonic plague.

In Christian Europe, where city streets doubled as sewers and where people were downright suspicious of bathing, the rats, the fleas and the plague all spread like wild fire.

You knew you were in trouble when a large boil appeared on your neck, armpit or groin. If it was lanced and thoroughly cleaned, you had a chance. If not, black spots started spreading over your skin. Then you began to cough and finally spit up blood. By that time you were highly infectious, and a contemporary would describe you as exuding an unbearable stench, "...sweat, excrement, spittle, breath so fetid as to be overpowering; urine turbid thick, black or red."

Who would hang around to nurse such a patient? Bernard Tolomei and his Benedictines of Mt. Olivet. Perhaps Bernard was crazy after all.

That's what peasants had reported to Church authorities years earlier when they charged that a group of madmen was inhabiting a wilderness area south of Siena. The charges were taken seriously enough that the madmen's leader was brought before the pope.

John XXII was impressed when he found out that Bernard was actually a nobleman of Siena who had been a soldier, a university scholar, and even a magistrate there. The pope learned that Bernard had just gotten fed up with the vanity of city life, and had sought the solitude of the hill country. His prayerfulness and serene example had attracted a few friends and thus the rumors.

The pope had Bernard and friends formalize their association by putting on religious garb and adopting the Rule of St. Benedict — about seventy or so instructions for those wishing to start a monastery dedicated to a balanced life of work, prayer and study.

They were still a relatively new group when the plague struck, but they had grown in numbers, and their work immediately began to include caring for the stricken. As the plague spread, eventually killing millions, they at first appeared miraculously immune. But finally one of their order was brought down on August 20th, 1348. It was Bernard himself, age 76.

Mt. Olivet rises among the jumbled hills about 25 miles south of Siena. Bernard never got to see the completion of the abbey's church or cloister but I'm sure he would have admired them, especially the cloister's thirty-six frescoes of scenes from the life of St. Benedict.

More than monks roam the hills of Southern Tuscany though. One spring, the special of the day at a local inn was listed as *cinghiale*. I had no idea what it was. So of course I ordered it right away. The others got chicken. The chicken was good. The *cinghiale* was outstanding — big chunks of dark rich meat roasted for hours in tomatoes, garlic, onion and beans.

On a stroll after dinner, we saw a butcher shop down the street plastered with signs touting *cinghiale, cinghiale.* No wonder it was so good; whatever it was was right in season. I hurried over to see stuck on a pole in the window all that was left of the shop's *cinghiale* — a big hairy head of a wild boar with his tongue drooping out and tusks jutting six inches up from his snout.

I ordered it again the next day with a rich local Chianti. One additional rule Bernard had tried to impose on his monks was abstinence from wine. Imagine, in Italy of all places. The pope was wrong. The peasants had Bernard pegged all along.

**Maybe
he
should
have
stayed at
home**

Years ago, I was a house father at a fraternity house near campus where young men lived who were considering studying for the priesthood. I smoked a lot then. (If you consider four packs a day a lot.) And I drank one pot of coffee each morning with my first pack while I was still waking up.

I was often criticized by indignant voices from the far end of the breakfast table for filling the kitchen with tobacco smoke, but I vigorously charged back that people were purposely blowing cereal fumes in my face.

There was no one to arbitrate. We could have used Louis IX.

This saintly king of France is remembered by many as an unsuccessful crusader, but historically he's more important perhaps as a law giver and administrator of justice. Sometimes he decided cases personally while leaning against an old oak tree in the forest of Vincennes. At other times, he dispatched special agents throughout France to insure that royal officials were acting justly and honorably especially in cases involving the rights of the poor or powerless.

His judges were forbidden to hang around taverns, gambling dens or houses of prostitution, and they were supposed to put an end to such ancient practices as ordeal by battle, in which cases were decided by who won out in a bloody duel or joust.

Furthermore, he established a supreme court, or parliament in Paris to review lower court decisions. The people of France came to believe that real justice and protection of their rights emanated from good King Louis.

Maybe he could have been happy with all that, but Louis had another dream. He wanted to "liberate" Jerusalem from the Moslem armies that had retaken it in 1244.

It was not an unreasonable goal. Louis was only 34, and had been commanding armies against foes like the English since he was 15. France itself was at peace, and his barons were willing to follow, if only reluctantly.

He entrusted the kingdom to his mother, Blanche of Castile. No worry there since the tough lady had ruled before for him when he first became king at the age of 12. He set out with over a hundred ships and 30,000 men on what became known as the Seventh Crusade.

But he didn't go to the Holy Land. Instead, he intended to capture lots of Egypt and then trade parts of it to the Sultan for Jerusalem and the areas around it. His plan worked at first. He landed on the coast, beat off the opposition, and headed toward Cairo itself.

But the Nile was at flood stage and months were lost. Finally, the French built a pontoon bridge and rushed the fortress of al-Mansurah. The battle lasted all day. Some say Louis won, others that he lost. At any rate, the French were exhausted and had to retreat, and eventually surrender.

Louis, the great king of France, was ill and a prisoner. His nation ransomed him for an enormous sum. He returned home in 1254, but he wouldn't give up his dream. At age 53, he tried again to take Egypt by a landing in Tunisia and marching east. The plague struck him down, and he died far from home.

His body was brought back to Notre Dame for his funeral Mass, and he was buried at the Abbey of St. Denis. His feast is celebrated August 25th.

MONICA AND AUGUSTINE

What's a mother to do?

ACT III - Scene Three
(Setting is in kitchen as older woman slides bacon and eggs from skillet onto plate, and younger man enters from right.)
Woman: Hurry and eat your breakfast son, or you'll be late for church.
Man: I don't want to go to church.
Woman: Don't be silly. Let's not have that argument again. You have to go to Mass.

Man: I don't want to go. It's always the same old prayers and the same old songs and the same old babies yelling the whole time. Give me one good reason why I have to go.

Woman: I'll do better than that. I'll give you three. You're 45 years old; you're the pastor; and if you don't get over to church, there won't *be* any Mass.

St. Monica did not live long enough to act out the above scene with her son Augustine. But she acted out plenty of others: the enraged parent, the hysterical widow, the manipulative schemer.

Augustine is justly famous as someone who had to struggle toward sainthood, but Monica's stumbling blocks are often overlooked. Her reputation for piety, for prayerfulness and for patient faith is well deserved. But Monica had her own demons to overcome too.

She came from a firmly middle class family of Tagaste in North Africa, a family proud of its Christianity but also protective of its respectability. The family saw no problem therefore in marrying their daughter off to a pagan named Patricius. He was a good catch — not overwhelmingly wealthy, but rich enough and of firm social standing in the town.

Monica had been raised rather strictly; so it appeared she would offer a good counterweight to the jolly, outgoing Patricius. Unfortunately, both had limitations as parents. Patricius pushed and pushed when it came to scholarship, but beyond that he let Augustine do practically anything he wanted. He was proud of showing off his son's obvious brilliance. Monica, for her part, spoiled the boy — instilling absolutely no self-discipline.

Her later concerns for Augustine's wild lifestyle would stem partly from guilt over this failure. Her other shortcomings included being more concerned for Augustine's respectability than for his true character, and of loving him with the utmost possessiveness.

Monica could not control the young Augustine, much less the grown teacher of rhetoric that he became. But she could preach at him: about God, about the family's reputation, about all the things she saw as important. So he tried to get away from her. After his father died, Augustine moved to Carthage. Monica followed — jealous of her son and envious of the mistress he had taken.

Augustine secretly moved on again — this time across the sea to Italy, and an outmaneuvered, enraged, hysterical Monica was left screaming at the pier.

In the midst of this abandonment, the defeated Monica underwent a great change. Alone, she turned to God for real solace, not for help in managing her son. Her faith took on more of the dimension of surrender to God's love and less of concern over propriety and respectability.

She did once more follow Augustine, but it was a different Monica who caught up with her son in Milan. Its famous bishop Ambrose remarked on her deep faith, her prayerfulness and wisdom, and her true love of others.

Monica lived to see her son's conversion to Christ, and his baptism by Ambrose, but she died on the way home to North Africa where her son would eventually become bishop. Her feast is celebrated on August 27th, and Augustine's the day after.

DRITHELM

You can have the valley. I'll take the plain

If you can write out your birth date on your next application for a credit card, you have Bede the Venerable to thank. No, he didn't invent pencils, but he did popularize the method of dating events in relation to their occurrence after the birth of Christ, i.e. Anno Domini, the Year of the Lord, A.D.

Before Bede's time, Europeans often dated things by relating them to a great disaster, or a ruling monarch, or a local event of some import. So people could be born in the fourth year after all the cows died, or in the tenth year of Philip the Bald's reign, or two years before lightning struck the abbot's ass.

It was all very confusing before Bede straightened things out. He had a selfish motive though. He needed a logical method of arranging happenings in order to write his *Church History of the English People*, the holy monk's account of events in Britain from the invasion of Julius Caesar up to his own time around the year 730.

Without Bede's history, we would be woefully ignorant of some fascinating saints that roamed merry ole England while it was still quite new.

Take Drithelm of Cunningham for example. Bede tells us almost all of what we know about him. It appears Drithelm isn't important so much for what he did while he was living, but for what he saw while he was dead.

Bede records that Drithelm was a good family man mourned by all on the night of his "death," who gave quite a fright to everyone when he arose the next dawn.

Only later, when Drithelm had become a penitent recluse did he tell worthy souls of his experience while dead. He told of a light, welcoming and peaceful, that came to greet him. But he also related some scary visions regarding those who failed to do good while alive.

He said that his guide led him to the edge of a valley where fearsome flames burned on one side and frigid cold cracked the very earth on the other. Drithelm watched as poor, dead souls took all they could of the heat and then ran to the other side of the valley. When they could stand the cold no longer, they vaulted back toward the flames.

He thought surely he was seeing hell. No, his guide assured him. Hell was much worse. The valley held those who repented from their sins, but only on the verge of death. As frightening as their predicament seemed, it was only temporary. They would gain salvation on the day of judgment.

Much more comforting is Drithelm's tale of a fragrant plain his guide led him to see. It was green and bright, and filled with happy people enjoying one another's company. Heaven? No again, his guide assured him, just another temporary abode, but this one for those who, though not perfect, tried to do good while living. They too awaited judgment day, but obviously without all the scurrying around of the valley people.

The dead traveler's feast is September 2nd.

CLODOALD

**Prince,
fugitive,
hermit,
hero,
saint**

In 496, Clovis, King of the Franks, was off to battle the Alamanni. He swore if he was victorious he would worship the god of his Christian wife Clothilde.

Clovis won out, and kept his promise. He was baptized on Christmas Day along with 3000 of his warriors. Perhaps they should have gone through RCIA first.

In the early days of the Roman Church, adults wanting to become Christian usually had to go through a long process of instruction and formation before baptism, a procedure known today as the Rite of Christian Initiation of Adults.

But sometimes on the fringes of the Empire, or when barbarian incursions disrupted settled ways of doing things, the process was reversed. Whole groups of pagans might be baptized all at once with the understanding that they could always go to catechism class later.

Imagine a Frankish warrior's surprise then when he learned that his new Christian faith meant not only that he had to cease worshiping his old gods, but that he had to quit dating his sister too.

Christianity for some became a thin veneer worn over more ancient, and often violent, ways of getting things done. Clovis himself died honorably, but the same can't be said of a lot of his descendants.

Of his three grown sons, the eldest tortured and killed the

saintly Burgundian king Sigismund, and was in turn murdered by avenging Burgundians who paraded his head around on a spike. Clovis' other sons then fell upon the eldest's heirs. Two they stabbed to death. Only five-year-old Clodoald escaped.

Who hid the child for fifteen years can only be guessed. His grandmother? Archbishop Remegius? The hermit Severin? Historians disagree on his location but not on the danger he was in as long as his uncles lived.

Clodoald would defeat his brothers' assassins but with weapons no one would have guessed.

When armed supporters learned of the prince's whereabouts, they flocked to him to swear loyalty and vow revenge. But his years as a fugitive had been a time of deep spiritual growth for Clodoald. Instead of an earthly kingdom, he wanted to seek the kingdom of God. He worshiped the Prince of Peace, not the gods of war.

In a dramatic gesture, he appeared within the safety of the cathedral of Paris wearing ermine robes and a sword, but carrying the simple frock of a hermit. Before the bishop and all assembled for worship, he renounced any claim to his father's throne, took off the trappings of royalty and disappeared wearing only the frock he had carried.

The people adored him. The further he would withdraw into a life of solitude and prayer to do penance for the sins of the world, the more they sought him out: for blessings, for prayers, for advice, and even for cures.

He could hide from his uncles but not from such adulation. After about ten years, he was brought to Paris by popular acclaim where believers insisted he be ordained.

"Father" Clodoald was then plunged into the busy life of active ministry. Even his uncles recognized his unique place in the hearts of the people, and, tired of dispatching assassins, sent money instead, lots of it. Clodoald gave it all away, to the poor, and to the Church, endowing Notre Dame itself.

After years of work in the city, he convinced the bishop to let him serve in the suburban village of Nogent. He became so loved there as a devoted pastor that after his death on September 7th, villagers renamed their district after their priest. You can visit his arm bone there today in St. Cloud as part of an excursion to nearby Versailles.

PETER CLAVER

Precious in the eyes of God's saints

1600 A.D. Europeans were enslaving and transporting about 4,000 Africans each year for work in the mines and fields of the New World. Later, the figure would grow to as many as 90,000 a year. It was not unusual for a slave ship to carry over 400 Africans, chained below deck with not enough room to even sit up.

Many never survived the trip, and those who did often landed diseased and starving after the 100 day ordeal.

But if they landed in Cartagena on the north coast of Colombia, at least one kind face was there to greet them — that of Peter Claver. He didn't speak their language, but he boarded every slave ship that landed with food, bandages, and a spirit of true humility, calling himself the slave of the slaves.

The young Jesuit from Spain had landed at the same dock himself in 1610, and worked among the sick and enslaved for forty-four years until his death.

As news of a ship's approach spread, Claver would go door to door collecting biscuits, brandy, tobacco and lemons to add to the stores he had already accumulated. He'd go on board with these to give to the Africans who were being brought up on deck, and then he would descend into the hold where urine and sweat, vomit and blood had collected for weeks.

Even his helpers often failed to go below with him, or

fainted when they did. Below lay those who could no longer get up. Claver bathed them, spoke in soothing though foreign tones to them, and gently kissed them. Peter Claver is not remembered for any effective renunciation of slavery, but instead for his personal love of the slave.

His work continued ashore. For slaves were then packed into camps or pens to await the market day on which they would be sold. Peter used interpreters and the aid of pictures to try to spread the message of a suffering Christ to those who were suffering the greatest indignities. He wanted to instruct and baptize as many as he could before they were dispersed to far off sugar plantations or island fields.

Later, he would travel on long missions to distant villages to preach, teach and administer the sacraments. Even after years of separation, his converts knew who he was as soon as they saw him.

But Peter Claver has to be seen as a man of his age. He knew the evil of slavery, but his message to the slave was the same as his message to the slave owner: God's love and mercy, and our need to repent. To Peter, even the slave needed reformation and renewal, even the slave needed to be contrite for his own sin.

In a sense, it was a vital recognition of the slave as not some dumb brute, as so many Europeans thought, but as a uniquely responsible soul made by a Creator common to all peoples.

Peter had a weird habit that possibly portrays this same idea. When slaves were in the last stages of leprosy, he would force himself to kiss their ugliest running sores. Maybe it was only Peter's way of enforcing a self-discipline to control his own instinctive tendency to avoid such horror — a further control of the will, a form of mortification.

But his 1935 biographer describes another motive:

Peter was acutely conscious of the need to restore self-respect to those whose very presence inspired normal people with disgust. And when he kissed their wounds the very extravagance of this gesture must have helped to convince the ulcerous lepers and infected slaves of the difficult truth that man is made in the image of God, and that the most degraded of lepers is infinitely precious in the eyes of God, and in the eyes of God's saints.

Peter Claver's feast is celebrated September 9th.

Pulcheria

An apple a day can get you killed

Nestorius, the Patriarch of Constantinople, had a heresy named after him — Nestorianism, the condemned belief that Jesus did not have two natures, one divine, one human. Oddly enough, Nestorius himself was probably not a Nestorian. He just got bad press.

One who brought about the downfall of what were *thought* to be Nestorius's beliefs was Pulcheria, the emperor's big sister: virgin, reformer, regent and a beautiful woman not to be fooled with.

When Emperor Arcadius of the Eastern Roman Empire died in 399, his son was still a child. So 15 year-old Pulcheria was made regent, and took over the boy's education, and the direction of life at the palace.

She was very serious about her Christianity and about her politics. She took a vow of chastity so that she could practice both without distraction.

Wild royal parties and lavish ceremonies were replaced with the singing of hymns and the chanting of psalms. Pulcheria's faith was not just for show though. She founded churches, endowed hospitals, and sewed clothes for the poor.

She saw that her little brother Theodosius learned his four "R's," the usual three, and religion too. She even endorsed the beautiful Eudocia as his young bride. And that was her first mistake.

Eudocia was a true match for her sister-in-law in looks, intelligence, and influence. The vacillating emperor found himself sometimes following the lead of his wife, and other times that of his sister. Even his role of leadership in the Church was affected.

Eudocia supported theologians who felt Christ had only one nature, his humanity being absorbed by his divinity. Pulcheria supported the pope in Rome and those who taught that Jesus was indeed divine, but totally human too.

Both encouraged the emperor to call Church councils to condemn one side or the other. Eudocia won round one. She got the emperor to force his sister into retirement away from court.

But Pulcheria left behind many old friends at court. It was perhaps they who helped bring about Eudocia's downfall. For a long time, some of them had gossiped that the emperor's best friend, Paulinus, was also the empress' "best friend."

A wonderful story has been preserved. On his way to church one day, Theodosius was given a huge apple, which he in turn sent to his wife, who in turn gave it to her friend Paulinus, who, thinking to please the emperor with such a fine fruit, gave it to Theodosius.

The emperor kept his cool. He merely proceeded to his wife's chambers where he asked her how she had liked the apple. Eudocia said it was delicious. Then Theodosius brought it out from under his cloak.

Imagine her embarrassment. She was disgraced. Imagine Paulinus's shock. He was assassinated.

Pulcheria's influence bounced back. Orthodoxy seemed ascendant. When Theodosius died in 450, Pulcheria became empress until her own death. She reigned for just a few years, but long enough to sponsor the Council of Chalcedon which proclaimed that Jesus was:

"truly God and truly man to be acknowledged in two natures without confusion, change, division, or separation."

Pulcheria's feast is celebrated September 10th. And what about Eudocia? She outlived her old rival, dying in Jerusalem where she had become loved for her own generosity and civic spirit.

Pesto, pesto, do your very besto

In a wonderful scene from the movie *Houseboat*, Sophia Loren gets into a shouting match with her father, an Italian diplomat representing his country in America. He wants her to go home. She refuses. He threatens to disown her. She vows to get a job.

"That's impossible!" he says. "I've given you the very best education in Europe. You don't know how to do anything."

"Very well then," she replies. "I'll run for Congress."

If such is the criterion, Joseph of Cupertino would have made a great senator. He failed as a shoemaker, was too clumsy to be a kitchen servant, and could learn only one topic as a student. Two religious houses turned down his application because he seemed so absentminded and untalented.

Finally, in 1620, the Franciscans accepted him as a lay brother in one of their monasteries. Joseph was never the same afterwards. As a matter of fact, neither were the Franciscans. For Joseph turned out to be outstanding in what they saw as holiness.

He was careful of his work in the stables, he was humble and kind, he willingly did penance for sin, and he was obedient to his spiritual advisors, and enjoyed mystical visions and raptures. Oh, and by the way, he could fly.

One of the earliest of his flights to be recorded occurred at Christmas. Joseph had invited some shepherds from the hills around Cupertino to come celebrate the feast with him. When he heard their approaching pipes and flutes, he began to dance with joy and religious ecstasy until he took off. When the shepherds arrived, they found him suspended in air between the middle of the church and the high altar.

There are over 100 stories about Joseph's flights thereafter, or what are sometimes called his levitations. But many of the stories are second hand and began to be circulated only after his death.

The account taken most seriously by investigators is the eyewitness tale of a Spanish admiral, his wife and aides and servants accompanying them on a visit to Assisi. Joseph had been moved there by the Franciscans, partly to keep him hidden away.

You see, his fame not only for levitation but for healing illnesses, foreseeing events, and offering solid counsel had made him quite a celebrity. Kings, dukes and prelates sought his advice and blessing, and a lot of ordinary people just wanted to see him fly. The Franciscans vacillated between being proud of Joseph and being embarrassed by him.

After the admiral had a private chat with Joseph, he talked to his wife who insisted on seeing him too. Joseph was told to go to the chapel to see her, and, ever obedient, he did. But when he came in, he was taken up in rapture to fly to the statue of Mary and then back down the aisle, over the heads of the admiral and everyone else, and out the door.

At a prayer service for Catholic law students, I was going to encourage them to pray to St. Joseph of Cupertino because when he was finally permitted to study for priesthood, it looked like he would flunk the final exam until the bishop just happened to ask him the one and only question he was prepared to answer, "What is the meaning of the biblical phrase, 'Blessed is the womb that bore thee'?"

I was going to remind the scholars of Joseph's place as

patron saint of students. But when I looked up the references, I found that that was not his principal listing. Instead, he's listed first as the patron saint of aviators. His feast is celebrated September 18th. However he's honored, I'm sure the humble Joseph's advice to both students and pilots would echo that of Sophia Loren sung to Cary Grant's kids:

> Pesto, pesto, do your very besto
> Bing bidda bing
> Bidda bing bang bong.

> They threw explosives at us but just for fun

Our darkened tour bus with its sleepy passengers wound peacefully along the Bay of Naples. Suddenly sharp explosions on the roof and under the chassis startled everyone awake. Those who had not drunk enough Lacrima Christi at dinner looked nervous and frightened. The delicious, amber-colored "Tears of Christ" kept the rest of us suitably calm as the guide explained what was going on.

It was only the children of Naples. They love to throw fire crackers and cherry bombs to enliven the visits of tourists. It was also New Year's Eve. So the crackle of fireworks continued all night.

The Neapolitans were celebrating another year in which volcanic Vesuvius had spared their city from its deadly rain of ash and molten lava.

Scientists might have pointed out that the last major blow was ninety years ago, but citizens knew that St. Januarius had come through for them once again.

Januarius is the patron saint of Naples. Little is known about him, but much is believed. He was one of the many Christian martyrs caught up in the persecution launched by the Roman Emperor Diocletian around the year 300.

In what is perhaps the single most unfortunate failure of the RCIA, the emperor's wife and daughter had dropped out of the program half way through. Not only were they no longer studying to be Christians, Diocletian even purged Christians from the imperial court.

The emperor had tolerated Christianity for a time but eventually saw it as weakening army discipline. Christian officers were refusing to wear some badges of rank because they bore likenesses of the emperor that proclaimed him divine. Anti-Christian propaganda might have swayed Diocletian too.

At any rate, edicts went out that ranged in severity from firing Christians from imperial service to "firing" them in a more literal sense. Enforcement of the edicts and their penalties varied from place to place and time to time.

Unfortunately, Januarius found himself in the wrong place at the wrong time. As bishop of Benevento, he felt obliged to visit one of his imprisoned deacons at Pozzuoli. He ended up being jailed himself and later decapitated.

But he's more fascinating dead than alive. His body was eventually brought to Naples where it was entombed in the main church of the city. Two vials of his blood, as well as his head, were also preserved. A great cathedral grew up around the tomb, and Januarius continued to be honored as a special patron of the city.

Then, in 1389, the vials of the saint's blood were being carried in procession around the cathedral when all of a sudden the centuries old coagulated masses began to soften, then liquefy, and even to bubble.

They've done that ever since, eighteen times a year, as a matter of fact, at least in good years. To a Neapolitan, a "bad" year is when the blood does not liquefy. And they point to subsequent periods of famine or war or pestilence to prove their point.

The vials are hermetically sealed and anchored inside thick crystal glass on both sides. On the appropriate dates, they are brought forward and held aloft while the faithful pray. And the phenomenon occurs.

Skeptical? Well if you can get to Naples by the 19th of September, the saint's feast, you can see for yourself.

Watch out for the cherry bombs, though.

CHAPTER IV

An uncontrollable urge

When I was finally ready to quit smoking, I signed up for an expensive clinic that was very successful in getting people to stop. I could smoke all I wanted but only in an airless, glass booth with a cord strapped to my arm that sent out a weak electrical current every time I lifted my elbow to inhale.

It worked. I overcame my nicotine addiction in one week. But ever since then, I sometimes have the uncontrollable urge to stick my big toe into empty lamp sockets.

Vincent de Paul had an uncontrollable urge too. His was nobler — to be of help to those in need.

That wasn't his primary goal at first. His parents were not wealthy, but they had enough money to get him through school. He must have been bright, because he was ordained a priest when he was only twenty, six years earlier than the norm. In France, priesthood then could be the road to greater wealth and an easier life than Vincent's brothers and sisters could hope for.

He seemed to be going down that road at first. He became a chaplain to the queen and to the wealthy de Gondi family, and he enjoyed an absentee benefice. That is, he received the income from the lands of a monastery he did not have to visit or have anything to do with really. Some of Vincent's fellow clergy even had several benefices they possibly never visited.

Vincent could have settled into the comfortable life of status and wealth enjoyed by important priests and bishops of his day. He was even respected by Cardinal Richelieu of *Three Musketeers* fame.

But a Father, later Cardinal, de Berulle seems to have steered Vincent in a different direction. De Berulle was interested in changing a prevailing notion that a person's salvation was their ultimate goal. This meant a lot of personal reformation, mortification, doing of penance, and so on. It was very individualistic.

De Berulle said that a Christian's ultimate goal was not individual salvation but simply the proclamation, glorification and adoration of God's majesty. How do we do this? Through Christ — by uniting ourselves to Christ, imitating Christ, seeing Christ in others. Vincent came to see what his friend meant.

And then he saw Christ in galley slaves chained to their oars, in infants abandoned in vast foundling homes, in peasants hungry for sound teaching and preaching, in the poor and the ill, and in refugees fleeing from war.

All these he helped, personally or through congregations of men and women he gathered together and organized with great skill and tenacity into nurses, preachers, teachers, missionaries, chaplains, and early social workers.

Vincent had a lasting effect not only in the organizations he founded, but in the inspiration his memory provided. He died September 27, 1660 when he was eighty. One hundred and seventy three years later, Frederic Ozanam founded the St. Vincent De Paul Society to imitate the saint's work. Ozanam himself was declared "Blessed" in 1977 at a special ceremony to celebrate his nomination for sainthood.

not abide fools, dissemblers or dim wits, and he was very hot tempered to boot. He would take offense easily, blow up at somebody, and then wail in remorse for his lack of self-control.

He left Rome after being secretary to the pope to withdraw to the Holy Land to conquer his pride and the cravings of the flesh, but he never mastered his tongue or reined in his pen.

After studying under the greatest theologians of the day, he settled into a monastery at Bethlehem at which he wrote and wrote and wrote — letters, pamphlets, theological treatises, translations of the Greek Fathers, and biblical commentaries such as his eighteen volumes on the prophet Isaiah alone. He was universally recognized as one of the great minds of the Church even by his enemies. And appeals for Jerome's opinion on doctrine frequently reached Bethlehem from all over.

But perhaps Jerome is best known for his work to arrive at an accurate and authentic translation of the whole Bible into Latin. While he was still at Rome, he had revised older Latin versions of the books of the New Testament, and at Bethlehem he undertook the translation of the Old.

It took him about fourteen years. He would not be satisfied with translating Greek texts or revising Latin editions. He went back to the Hebrew Scriptures instead. His combined work came to be known as the Vulgate — the official Bible of the Western Church declared so by the Council of Trent over a thousand years after Jerome's death on September 30, 420. Older Catholics may recall reading from an English version of the Vulgate, a translation made at Douay and Rheims in France.

Jerome was admired, respected and often roundly hated. But at least he was astutely aware of his own shortcomings and confessed them dramatically. He is sometimes painted in an act of mortification, beating his breast with a rock. When Pope Sixtus V once passed such a painting, he remarked, "You do well to carry that stone, Jerome, for without it the Church would never have canonized you."

POPE PIUS V

Holy Mother of God, smash the Turks

When the Turkish sailors saw their young admiral's head paraded on a Christian pike, some understandably lost heart. The battle for their ship had been going on for two hours, but the preparations for that day had taken months.

Pope Pius V had at last convinced Spain and Venice to join him in a Holy League to resist Turkish expansion into Europe by attacking the Sultan's fleet. They could strike a blow for Christianity against Islam, and at the same time, free thousands of Christian galley slaves rowing in Turkish warships.

In 1571, the Holy League fleet of over 200 ships powered by sail and its own slaves left Italy for the western coast of Greece, and came up against almost 300 galleys of the Sultan near their port of Lepanto.

Neither side hesitated to charge right at the other. One Turkish wing got to the rear of the Christians' northernmost squadron and the fight was on. Christian muskets, powerful but slow, killed Turks, while Turkish cannon and poisoned-tipped arrows killed Christians.

The archers fired faster, and lots of Spaniards and Venetians fell, but you had to grapple and board your opponent to win the fight, and in this hand-to-hand combat, the odds were more even.

In the center, Admiral Ali Pasha on his flagship "Sultana"

led his four hundred men right at Admiral Don Juan aboard the "Reale." The Christian leader had exactly the same idea.

The two warships collided, and the shooting, stabbing, hacking and gouging commenced. Both admirals had planned for just such an engagement, and additional galleys on both sides latched on to the rear of their commanders' ships and started pouring reinforcements aboard.

First, it looked like the "Reale" would be taken. Then the Christians pushed their attackers back onto the decks of the "Sultana." Back and forth the slaughter went on.

But the superbly trained Spanish infantry finally began to wear down the Turks. Because there were so many large ships latched together, the center of this naval engagement actually resembled a land battle. Except of course to those who drowned overboard.

Toward the end, Don Juan himself was slipping in blood as he and his men slowly made progress down along the deck of the "Sultana." The admiral was swinging a broadsword in one hand and an axe in another.

His counterpart was letting arrows fly from the stern until an harquebus ball landed in the center of Ali Pasha's head, which was promptly cut off and then hoisted aloft.

The remaining Turks gave way. Other Turkish galleys lost similar fights all around the bay, and only about 30 were able to retreat into Lepanto's harbor. It was about 5:00 in the evening, October 7th.

Hundreds of sea miles away, Pius was going over some financial reports with his treasurer-general. He suddenly stopped talking, got up, and went over to look out the window.

After a moment, he turned around, his normally ashen face bright with joy, and exclaimed, "God be with you! This is not the time for business. Let us give thanks to Jesus Christ, for our fleet has conquered."

The aged and dying Pius had previously been fasting three days a week, and had promulgated that all believers should pray the Rosary fervently for the success of the Holy League.

Once the fleet had sailed, he redoubled his own prayers, and committed its safety to "Our Lady Queen of the Most Holy Rosary."

On October 21st, messengers arrived to confirm the pope's vision. He praised Don Juan and all his men, but attributed the victory to prayer, and declared October 7th a day of thanksgiving that would eventually be called the Feast of the Holy Rosary.

Cervantes was wounded at Lepanto, but lived to give his view on the power of prayer in *Don Quixote*. Much later, G.K. Chesterton perhaps tried to capture some of the old pope's apprehension in his poem "Lepanto":

> The pope was in his chapel before day or battle broke,
> (*Don John of Austria is hidden in the smoke.*)
> The hidden room in a man's house where God sits all the year,
> The secret window whence the world looks small and very dear.

BRIDGET OF SWEDEN

St. Catherine's mom was a saint too

A friend of mine told me that at his parish, when the Masses get too crowded, the pastor makes everyone hold hands during the Our Father. The crowds melt away for awhile until word gets out that they don't have to hold hands anymore.

We have one Mass that's too crowded here. So I was thinking of resorting to that idea. But then I thought, "Wait a minute. Some folks like to hold hands at the Our Father. What if word gets around that that's the Mass to get to if you like that practice? I could end up with a condition in which the latter state is worse than the first."

For there is just no accounting for taste where prayer is concerned. Take St. Bridget of Sweden for example. Her dramatic visions provided her with scenes of Christ's passion which she then translated into prayers of vivid and graphic detail. Just a few examples:

O Jesus, heavenly physician, remember
the languor, lividness and pain which Thou
didst suffer on the lofty scaffold of the
Cross, torn in all Thy limbs, not one of which
remained in its right state.
O sweet Jesus, true and fruitful vine, remember
the overflowing and abundant effusion of blood,
which poured in torrents, like wine pressed from
the grape, when on the press of the Cross Thou didst

tread alone.
Thy delicate flesh faded,
the moisture of Thy members and the marrow of Thy
bones dried up.

Does St. Bridget's style of prayer have wide appeal today?
I don't know. But I do know that her concern for the needy,
for social justice, for reform in the Church, for raising children
in the faith can still provide great inspiration for Catholics everywhere.

The Swedish Sankta Birgitta was born to wealth and married wealth, but was never its prisoner. Instead she used her
resources to help those in need, and to provide for her beloved
husband and eight children an excellent example of both personal aid to the poor and work for social reform.

She often took the kids with her on visits to the hospital
she supported to nurse, bathe and comfort patients of all social classes, and she worked with her husband for legal reforms
to protect the powerless.

When Ulf died in 1344, Bridget withdrew to a monastery
where she planned a quiet life of penance and prayer. But her
continued mystical revelations guided her back to court and
the wider world where she urged moral reform upon a lax king
and a worldly set of nobles.

She then felt called to go to Rome to try to bring about
reconciliation between the papacy which was away in Avignon
and the Holy Roman Emperor. Her calls to reform and renewal
were buttressed by dire prophecies should she go unheeded.

One who accompanied her on pilgrimages and peace missions was her own daughter, Catherine. Catherine got to tes-
tify in favor of her mother's canonization which took place
October 8th, 1391. Later, Bridget's feast was moved to July 23rd.

Pope Pius XI of Catholic Action fame kept a portrait of a
beautiful woman on his desk to inspire him, one of the mystical Swede.

> **How many Poles does it take to find their country on a map?**

Despite being an energetic and intelligent people, no amount of Poles could find their nation on a map in 1795. In a sleight of hand surpassing the trickiest magician, Austria, Russia and Prussia had made Poland disappear, dividing its territory among themselves.

When Angela Truszkowska was born in 1825, her parents lived in the Russian sector. She confronted serious illness at birth, conquered tuberculosis at sixteen, and outwitted the Czar at forty.

Her noble family was wealthy enough to have a house in the city and a small estate in the country, and her parents encouraged her to join in the social scene at winter balls and summer picnics.

But she was quieter than most and a little more serious. She was deeply religious as a child, and wondered for a time if she was called to the cloistered life.

Instead, she eventually found herself busy as the head of a rapidly growing religious Order caring for orphans, running hospitals, and making home visits to the poor.

First, it had been just she and a cousin teaching catechism to village children in a small church near her parents' summer home. Then, they started sponsoring orphans back in Warsaw in the winter.

It actually became fashionable for young "belles" to abandon their balls and work with abandoned children instead. Angela was joined first by a dozen, then by dozens more. They donned the religious habit of the Franciscans, and soon were running hospitals and orphanages, and teaching in twenty-seven schools.

But the nuns weren't only angels of mercy, they were Polish patriots too. When their countrymen rose in revolt, they nursed the wounded in their hospitals. And when the revolt was shattered, they hid the defeated in their convents.

One police search failed to find a Polish soldier authorities swore was in her own convent because Mother Superior Angela Truszkowska had personally hidden him in a garbage can under a pile of bloody bandages from the hospital laundry.

The young soldier fainted in the can, but lived to praise the Sisters. Praise was far from what the Czar had in mind though. In retaliation for their aid to the rebellion, he disbanded Angela's Sisters, and they had to disperse among the homes of relatives and friends.

Angela wasn't the type to give up. It took her a lot of time and effort, but she eventually won Emperor Franz Joseph's consent for her Order to work in the Austrian sector of Poland. She got word to her Sisters to gather by ones and twos in Kraków, and soon, they were up and running again.

Angela liked to pace back and forth in front of a portrait of her special patron, St. Anthony, praying alone or talking to the saint. Some thought that years of hard work had finally taken their toll on her mind, especially when they overheard her scolding Anthony for not yet finding a new suit for a penniless, young student. He would not be permitted to take his final university exams unless he was suitably dressed.

Her friends needn't have worried about Angela. Minutes later, a businessman showed up at the convent door to donate a new suit some "foolish tailor" had crafted too small.

As her age advanced, Angela slowed her work. But she lived long enough to see the first group of her Sisters depart for America to work among Polish immigrants in the New World.

She had been baptized in her crib because the doctor did not think she would live out the week. Instead, she just about lived out the century, dying on October 10th, 1899, at the age of 74.

A hungry tourist abroad

On the way to Westminster Abbey in London, I stopped off at what was either the oldest or the smallest bakery in England. I forget which. Unfortunately, their pastries could have fit either description.

At least I think a pastry was what I ate, but it might have been a sandwich because the word chalked on their board was very confusing, naming something we would expect to see only in a burlesque show. The whole trip had been going that way for the last few days.

A friend and I had rented a flat for one week to save on the cost of hotel and restaurant bills. All went well until he knocked over a metal lamp in his room and broke it. He decided to go to a hardware store down the block to see if they could fix it before the owners came back.

I waited for a long time, and finally went to see what was going on. When I got to the store, he was yelling at the clerk, "A gair age in the mews? A gair age in the mews? What's a gair age in the mews?" I piped in that a mews was something like an alley.

"OK," he said, "Then what in God's name is a gair age?" Exasperated, the clerk took him by the elbow, out the store, to the corner of the alley where he pointed down the mews to a sign that read "Blythe's Garage and Welding Shop."

English just has too many words and too many ways to

spell them and pronounce them. I blame St. Edward the Confessor for a large part of the problem.

Edward became king of England after it had been ruled by Danes for a time. Cousins in Normandy had sheltered and supported him in exile until their forty-year-old relative went home to rule.

Edward was kind. He was cautious. He was benevolent. He was just. Unfortunately, he was also childless. When he died in January of 1066, he was already well on his way to being recognized as a saint, and England was well on its way to being invaded by his mother's kin from across the channel.

The English Anglo-Saxons and Danes favored Harold Son of Godwine as the native son candidate for the crown, but William of Normandy had other ideas. He fought and won the day at Hastings.

I once told a former teacher of mine that Harold was probably demoralized and defeated even before the battle began because he had heard that William had gotten the pope to excommunicate him for "usurpation." My teacher agreed, but added that an arrow through Harold's eye toward the end of the battle was certainly a contributing factor too.

Edward went on to canonization and the English language went on to become part French when it was already a mixture of Latin, Anglo-Saxon, and Norse with some Celtic remnants lying around. Edward's feast day is October 13th. He began the construction of Westminster Abbey in which he is buried, in which William the Conqueror was crowned, and in which I digested either my pastry or my sandwich.

Was it
religious
zeal or
just lack
of
prudence?

On October 19th, the Church honors six
Jesuit priests and two lay volunteers, missionaries to North America who were
killed on the job:

René Goupil, murdered with an ax.

Isaac Jogues, decapitated.

John Lalande, tomahawked.

Antoine Daniel, pierced by arrows.

Charles Garnier, shot twice, then tomahawked.

Nöel Chabanel clubbed down by a disgruntled convert.

John de Brébeuf and Gabriel Lallemant, tortured to death.

Why didn't they just leave the Indians alone?

The answer to that lies at the very core of Christianity.
Unlike quieter religions, its nature is to propagate itself. From
its earliest beginnings, believers have felt called to not only
profess the faith, but to spread it too.

The first generation of Jesuits took that calling very seriously. The next generation maybe took it to extremes.

In the 1500's, missionaries like Francis Xavier endured
all necessary hardships to spread the Gospel. But Francis himself had encouraged Jesuits in America to be prudent in just
how they expended their lives in God's service.

French Jesuits of the 1600's, though, came here *looking*
for trouble. All but one, at one time or another, had expressed
a desire to suffer martyrdom. Not a willingness, a desire.

When Isaac Jogues, for example, was asked by the Jesuits why he wanted to become one of them, he responded, "To go to Ethiopia to die." He was told, "No, you will go to New France to die."

Even if they were less prudent than Francis, they were certainly as heroic in their willingness to confront lengthy and rigorous canoe trips; live in wretched and extreme conditions; work among suspicious villagers far from other missionaries; coax along the rare and reluctant convert; and constantly be on guard for the blow that could come at any time.

And this was among friendly tribes.

For being French meant that some tribes were very, very unfriendly toward them. The French colonial powers had long before sided with the Algonquins against the Mohawks, and gave the Hurons, not the powerful Iroquois, the best of the fur trade.

It became routine for the Iroquois and their British allies to compete against the French and the Hurons in peace time, and to confront them aggressively in war. And there was very little peace, and a whole lot of war.

The Catholic missionaries found themselves hindered and endangered, caught up in the trade rivalry of global colonial powers. Jogues preached among the Hurons, suffered torture under the Mohawks, was rescued by the Dutch, and dispatched by the French on a peace mission to the Iroquois.

The tenacity of the missionaries, their fearless zeal, won them respect, and won converts to Christ. But the European diseases they and the traders carried also brought death. And the metal axes and tools they taught the Hurons to use made the Indians ever more dependent on the fur trade required to buy these imported novelties.

From war, famine, and sickness, the number of Christian Indians shrank and shrank. Were the missionaries disappointed with the results of their efforts? While retreating hundreds of miles to the safety of Quebec with just a few hundred remaining Huron Christians, Father Paul Ragueneau wrote:

> It was not without tears that we quitted the country that owned our hearts and held our hopes, which had already been reddened by the glorious blood of our brethren, which promised us a like happiness and which opened to us the road to Heaven and the gate of Paradise. *Mais quoi!* One must forget self and relinquish God's interests for God's sake.

CRISPIN AND CRISPINIAN

Knights in armor brought down by cobblers?

Having been a priest for almost twenty-five years, and having survived the implementation wars of Vatican II, I am no stranger to Church disputes or a good rollicking fracas in the name of religion. But a first occurred the other day. A parishioner called the police on me.

I was dressed in my black suit and headed out the front door of the rectory for a 10:30 funeral when I ran into a uniformed officer on the front porch. He asked me if there was a Charles Thomas around. I 'fessed up, and he told me that he had had a complaint phoned in about a Buick station wagon registered in that name and parked right in front of church in defiance of the "No Parking-Funeral" signs set out early that morning.

I immediately plea-bargained. The funeral was to be led by an out-of-town director who wouldn't have any "No Parking" signs with him. I purposely put the big old Buick wagon out to save room for the hearse. Then, I put blue trash barrels upside down along the street to save as many other places as I could on the busy thoroughfare in front of the church.

After sunrise, a kindly local funeral director brought his signs down, and I removed the barrels. Unfortunately, I forgot about my car, and the parishioner who phoned the authorities had no idea whom he was turning in. At least I think he didn't.

I got off with just a mild request from the officer to please move the car. Too bad Crispin and Crispinian didn't meet with that kind of official. They encountered a sadistic maniac instead.

The two brothers were said to be noble Romans who came north to Gaul where they spread the Gospel by day and worked at night as shoemakers to support themselves. Their martyrdom seems certain but its location is unsure. Maybe it was only their bones that made the trip north.

The best story has them being arrested during the persecution of Diocletian and his co-emperor Maximian around 286. Maximian tried bribes and threats to get them to forsake their faith, but they refused. So he turned them over to the cruel prefect Rictiovarus.

Rictiovarus first tortured them on the rack. Then he had millstones tied around their necks and threw them in the river. When the strong cobblers swam to the opposite bank, the enraged prefect built a great fire and threw them in it. When the fire refused to consume them, Rictiovarus was so beside himself that he jumped in the conflagration after them.

The fire didn't spare him. Nor did Maximian spare the shoemakers. He had them beheaded. The French claim the brothers are buried at Soissons, but Germans at Osnabruck and Italians in Rome insist they have part of their relics. Perhaps the English provide the best ending to Crispin and Crispinian though. An old story there says their bodies were thrown into the sea and ended up across the channel.

Both English and French cobblers claim Crispin and his brother as patrons. Who has the stronger claim? I'm not sure. But it is a fact that on October 25th, 1415 the former smashed the latter at Agincourt on Shakespeare's Henry V's famous "St. Crispin's Day."

JOHN OF CAPISTRANO

Just how poor is poor?

Every year on the feast of St. Joseph, observers in California watch for delicate swallows to return to San Juan Capistrano. Eagles would be more appropriate if you believe Capistrano's friends, vultures if you believe his enemies.

John of Capistrano fought heretics, Turks and his fellow Franciscans with zeal, courage and a fiery eloquence. His call to religious life came as another of those prison conversions. It occurred while he was in jail for helping the citizens of Perugia overthrow their government.

He never did anything half-heartedly. He sided with the Franciscans who took their vow of poverty very seriously, and argued against those who thought it was OK to amass worldly wealth in order to pursue their spiritual goals.

For years, his fame as a reformer and an inspiring preacher spread all throughout Italy, and brought him to the attention of several popes who employed him as an inquisitor, a diplomat, and eventually as the leader of a crusade.

In 1451, when John was 65, he was sent north to Bohemia and Hungary as part of a preaching mission to revive the Catholic faith and to convince believers to avoid the heresies of a condemned Czech named Jan Hus.

Great crowds turned out to hear him. He rose before dawn, preached most of the day wherever folks could gather, and made the rounds visiting the sick.

215

His Franciscan friends back in Italy wanted him home though. Their branch of the Order was in danger of being suppressed. They had insisted that radical poverty was an essential part of following in the footsteps of St. Francis, and so were besieged by the Franciscan establishment. They were threatened with ouster or with forced reunification with the rest of the Franciscan family.

John was their best preacher and strongest advocate. He had had the ear of popes and emperors. Surely he would come home to champion their cause.

But in the most painful decision of his life, John said, "No." A crisis was brewing in the north and he had to stay where he was.

Mohammed II was moving on Christian Belgrade with a vast Moslem army and a fleet sailing up the Danube. The Hungarians were willing to resist, but disorganized. Some of the Serbs wanted to cut a deal with the Turks if they would pass on through and go straight for Italy. The Czechs, Croatians and others agreed to fight but made no move to actually field an army.

The great preacher then turned his talents to war mongering, inciting Christians to the danger that threatened all Europe if the "infidel" got past Belgrade.

Even General Hunyadi, the Hungarian field marshal, wanted to give up the city, but by then John had gathered a few thousand crusaders to defend the walls. He rallied them with a banner of the cross that he waved from the parapets as the enemy came on.

The Turks broke through in several places. Hunyadi withdrew the regular garrison to safety across the river. The drawbridge was about to fall. But John of Capistrano, intoning, "Jesus, Jesus, Jesus," waved his banner and urged the defenders on.

Then an incident occurred that almost cost John his saint-hood, since it was brought up against his case when his canonization was later discussed.

It seems a Turk had mounted the wall only to be grabbed by a fierce Hungarian. The Hungarian asked John if his soul would be saved if he jumped to his death off the wall with the Turk in his grip. In so many words, John said, "Sure, go ahead." And over the wrestlers went.

John's tenacity saved Belgrade, but the retreating Turks left the disease of rotting corpses in their wake. One of its victims was an already aged and exhausted John of Capistrano. He died more peacefully than he lived on October 23rd at the age of 69.

A bent halo

I was scheduled to attend a conference on stewardship with the priest from the neighboring parish. I thought I could demonstrate some good stewardship by going one day later to get a cheaper flight, taking the extra bed in the room *his* parish was paying for, and just *sneaking* into the conference, which I found very expensive but not very well guarded.

Of course I felt guilty being where I was not supposed to be. So I only stayed a minute or two. The fact that charming and intriguing New Orleans lay just beyond the convention center doors, basking in eighty-two degrees of summer sunshine, may have had something to do with my moral decision-making.

In between visits to restaurants, cafes and bakeries, I managed to tour some of the French Quarter. When I stopped at St. Louis Cathedral, a very kind guide took me on a private tour of the place since no crowds of tourists were occupying her time.

When I asked her if the diocese was planning any major celebrations for All Saints Day, she told me that actually the city's cemeteries, not its churches, are the real focus of attention that day, as folks visit the graves of loved ones they hope are numbered among all the unofficial saints honored November 1st.

Perhaps Pope Gregory IV was thinking of paying tribute to some of his dead relatives when he declared All Saints Day a universal feast in the Church in 837. Parts of the Church had already been honoring "all known and unknown" saints on that day for some time, thus being sure nobody missed their just due.

When Catholics in New Orleans honor undeclared saints on All Saints Day, I wonder if any of them think of Father Antonio de Sedella, better known as Père Antoine.

Father Anthony came to Louisiana from his native Granada in 1779 because his Capuchin religious Order was replacing French priests with Spanish priests after the territory had gone to Spain following the French and Indian War.

His intelligence and brilliant preaching helped him rise to be rector of the Cathedral in just a few short years, and his prominence seemed assured. Then, the governor sent him packing. He had learned that Father Anthony had been appointed to lead the Inquisition in Louisiana, and the governor wouldn't tolerate any such institution that might hamper business or interfere with trade or immigration.

A humbler Father Anthony returned from Spain three years later to take up his post at the cathedral again, where he remained as pastor, sometimes officially, sometimes unofficially, until his death at the age of 81.

Père Antoine was the "unofficial" pastor off and on because he simply couldn't get along with Church authorities, who suspended him at least twice. When Father Patrick Walsh, the administrator of the diocese in between bishops tried to wrest control of the cathedral from Père Antoine, the lay trustees and parishioners raised such a fury that Walsh withdrew the rest of the clergy from St. Louis and designated a convent chapel down the street as the new parish church.

When Bishop John Carroll of Baltimore dispatched a new

bishop to New Orleans after it had become part of the United States, Père Antoine got into a fight with him, too. The bishop had to place his own cathedral under interdict and suspend the feisty Spaniard.

The people always stood by Father Anthony. The new American might be bishop, but "The Père" was their pastor, beloved for his simplicity, his care for the poor, and his devoted service to his parish. When he died in 1829, his funeral was the largest the city had ever seen. Black bunting hung from public buildings, ships in the harbor flew their flags at half mast, and the whole French Quarter was draped with dark crêpe.

If you visit Père Antoine's Cathedral, go on the first, not Halloween. For there are fifty-two lay people buried under its main aisle, and if that's not scary enough, there are seven bishops entombed under its altar.

CHARLES BORROMEO

> **They tried to kill him once, or maybe twice**

Charles Borromeo wasn't much to look at. Though his mother was a Medici, he inherited none of her family's good looks or charm.

He wasn't much to listen to, either. A speech defect plagued him from childhood, and even as a cardinal archbishop he spoke slowly and too softly to be easily heard. But his indomitable will and tireless spirit made him the champion of all who sought reform in the Church and the scourge of those who opposed it.

His ability for careful organization and his methodical application to detail helped him rise to administrator of the diocese of Milan and papal Secretary of State when he was still in his twenties. Of course, the fact that his uncle was the pope may have helped, too.

When the final session of the Council of Trent convened in 1562, Borromeo was there to guide its work of reform. He was part diplomat, part politician, part theologian. He counted votes, shored up allies, lobbied interest groups. He set agendas, rearranged sessions, and bolstered flagging spirits.

When Trent outlawed many of the abuses that had led to the Protestant Reformation, a renewed Church had Bishop Charles Borromeo to thank. His reward, however, was to go to his own diocese of Milan to try to enforce the Council's reforms in the real world.

He started by paying decent salaries to his own household and forbidding them from accepting "presents" from anyone who had business with the bishop. He saw that his clergy were trained in ritual and educated in theology, and he insisted on Sunday schools in every parish so that the faithful could come to really understand the Faith.

He ousted pastors who didn't measure up and started to reform those monasteries and religious Orders who pursued worldly wealth over spiritual riches. And this led him into mortal danger.

When the priests of Santa Maria della Scala claimed an ancient exemption from the authority of the bishop and his reforms, Borromeo personally set out for their church on an inspection tour.

He arrived in full vestments carrying his episcopal cross on high. Had anyone laid out coffee and doughnuts? Was the bishop invited in for dinner and maybe a game of cards with the guys? No. The door was slammed in his face and shots rang out, zinging over his head and banging into his cross.

He eventually prevailed over the priests at della Scala, and over a group called the Humiliati too. They had started as a reforming religious Order in the 12th century, took up the wool trade to support themselves and became very, very rich.

They were few in number by Borromeo's time, but their leaders lived in palaces scattered around the diocese. They didn't think much of the bishop's ideas about cleaning up their act and moving back to their monasteries.

Some of the monks came up with an excellent solution. They hired a hit man.

Imagine a cool Wednesday evening in the fall. Vespers are concluding in the bishop's crowded little chapel. He's kneeling at prayer, listening to the choir intone the angel's farewell words to Tobias from the Old Testament, "It is time therefore that I return to Him who sent me."

With a superb sense of timing the assassin fires from behind the doorway, and the bishop slumps to the ground, already commending himself to the judgment of a merciful God. But a bishop's vestments back then weren't anything if not thick. The layers of cloth blunted the shot, and Borromeo ended up with just a bad bruise.

His bravest moments though weren't in dodging bullets, but in confronting something far more deadly in his day. In 1576, the plague struck Milan.

The governor fled, the nobility took off, city magistrates left town. The bishop shamed them all. He turned his great organizational skills to fighting the disease. He expanded hospitals, started up soup kitchens, rationed food supplies, housed volunteers in his own house, and personally took the sacraments to hundreds of the dying.

The bishop cheered his friends and gravely disappointed his enemies by surviving the plague. But he may have worn himself out in other ways, because he died on November 4th, 1584, when he was only 46, or about the age at which American priests sometimes become bishops today.

POPE LEO THE GREAT

The scourge of God meets the vicar of Christ

Attila the Hun may have been fierce; many conquered people referred to him as the Scourge of God. He may have been ruthless; he did murder his own brother so that he could rule alone. And he certainly may have been ugly; a lot of ancient chronicles agree on that.

But he wasn't invincible. His huge army was defeated by a smaller force of Romans, Gauls and Goths in what is now part of France. He expected to make his last stand the next day, and even had all his army's stores and baggage piled in a giant heap for burning.

But the Roman commander had gone off in another direction to settle some internal political dispute among the allies, and Attila escaped with what was left of his horde and headed south for Italy. There of course he sacked, looted, pillaged and burned — until, that is, he met Pope Leo in 452.

One story of their meeting has the long dead Peter and Paul appearing in Attila's camp hovering behind Leo and his priests, so that the superstitious Hun took fright and then flight.

Certainly having ghostly apostles on your side in any discussion would buttress your negotiating points. But Leo was also a skilled diplomat and bargainer in his own right. When the Vandals invaded Rome a few years later, Leo could not save the situation entirely, but he got them to agree not to burn the city, and to be discriminate in just how many they massacred.

Leo gets into the history books for just such exploits, but he's interesting and important for other reasons too. He's called a Doctor of the Church for combining sanctity with great learning and instruction. The Church still has about ninety of his sermons and some one hundred of his letters to bishops, monks, emperors and councils.

They portray a firm leader who was moderate in his treatment of persons, but forceful in his support or condemnation of movements and ideas.

He upheld the position that Jesus was both truly divine and truly human, and called the Council of Ephesus a Robber Synod for not being clear and unmistakable on that point.

He also lectured against holdover pagan practices such as honoring December 25th as the Birth of the New Sun instead of celebrating it as the birth of *God's* Son.

Another title he holds is "The Great." Not many popes are given that suffix. Leo perhaps possesses it because he was so instrumental in strengthening the position that the pope of Rome is the true successor to St. Peter.

He built up that notion administratively by organizing the Church from the top down, and by dispatching diplomats to represent his views around the empire. But he also tried to give it theological foundation by insisting on his personal belief that Jesus did indeed work directly through him as his Vicar on Earth.

Finally, he might be compared to Pope John Paul II in his insistence on the dignity of the human person. Leo felt that all believers had an inherent worth given them by Christ, and that grace was added to this worth so that they could love what God loves and refrain from doing what displeases the Master.

Leo died on November 10th, 461. He had tried to keep the Roman empire in the West from crumbling. In this, he failed. But he succeeded in building up an international institution that in many ways would take its place.

He also outlived Attila, who died long before from a burst blood vessel. Some say it happened on the night of his wedding to a beautiful Gothic maid named Hilda. His empire dissolved, and his bride went down in history as a notoriously poor judge of character.

Some commentators nowadays refer to this or that politician as being to the right of Attila the Hun. Perhaps the country would be better served if more leaders positioned themselves squarely in the tradition of Leo instead.

ALBERT THE GREAT

When my friend knocked himself out in Budapest, I almost missed the mid-morning bouillon served on the afterdeck. I told him he was too tall for his speed.

The "Mozart" is a beautiful barge, outfitted with a great restaurant and spacious staterooms, but being European, its doorways are too short. Tall, slow Americans have no problem, but those in a hurry are constantly banging their heads coming aboard. After a brisk morning walk along the Danube, that's exactly what my companion did.

I missed the whole thing until I saw waiters running away from the bouillon and hot cocoa carts as I was hurrying toward them. I turned around to ask my friend what all the panic might be about, and there he lay, sprawled on the gangway.

St. Albert the Great had the same problem. He was too quick a giant for his age. He was describing the earth as a sphere 250 years before Columbus ever set sail.

Albert was born not too far from where my friend was unconsciously delaying my snack, in Lauingen, upriver from the "Mozart"'s berth. His wealthy parents thought they had secured a bright future for him when they sent him south to Padua to study. Little did they know his own brightness would illumine the future itself.

At Padua, he was taken with the intellect and the holiness of the new Dominican leader, Jordan of Saxony. Albert became one of the ten students Jordan recruited to the recently formed order of mendicant friars — those not tied to any one monastery but free to be sent to wherever they were needed, and called to make their way by their own work and wit.

Albert made his way, studying, teaching, writing — to Paris, to Cologne, to the court of the pope, and to his own cathedral as a bishop in Germany. Along the way, he picked up a brilliant student of his own, Thomas Aquinas.

Before Aquinas, it was Albert who sought to reconcile the richness of his faith with all that his reason could teach him. New translations of Aristotle were available at the University of Paris, and Albert studied every work of the Great Philosopher he could lay his hands on. He wrote commentaries on all Aristotle's works and on all kinds of works that weren't really Aristotle's after all.

He comprised an entire encyclopedia of human knowledge, using the wisdom of the ancients and the teachings of the Faith, but also careful observation, scientific analysis, and sound reasoning. Pope John Paul II's recent remarks about science and faith reaching the one undivided truth could easily have been lifted from the work of this man called "Magnus" — The Great — already in his own lifetime.

Such a great honor didn't mean everyone agreed with Albert. Slower, smaller minds were headed in different directions. His last long journey was a sad one. He had to go to Paris and back during his retirement in Cologne. His prize pupil was dead, and university professors were attacking Aquinas' work.

When a young monk tried to talk the 77-year-old scholar from such a long journey on foot, Albert told him:

> I must go. Thomas is dead and cannot defend himself. Others who gladly would speak for him are dead. I have little left to give. But I am grateful that

God has spared me to go once more to the defense
of so great a man.

Albert made the journey and lived three more years, dying November 15, 1280.

I think his keen intellect and sense of observation would
have noticed that the bouillon, though lacking in its accident
of "hotness" by the time my friend had been revived, had retained its ontological essence completely.

Elizabeth of Hungary

What she had in her hamper was a thorny subject

At age 25, typical candidates for the priesthood still have another year to go; most law students haven't yet passed the bar; and aspiring doctors are still in medical school. When *she* was 25 years old, however, Elizabeth of Hungary had already been dead for a year.

But she had packed a lot of living into her short life, and a good head start had helped — she got engaged when she was four.

She was married at 14, a mother of three and a widow at 20, dead at 24, and a canonized saint when she would have been 28.

All her brief life, she had been known for kindness and charity. As a royal princess of Hungary and the wife of the wealthy ruler of Thuringia, she could certainly afford to be generous. But Elizabeth's charity was personal.

Not only did she throw open royal granaries during times of famine, she also passed loaves of bread to hundreds of individuals. She learned the names of the people she gave her own clothes to, and she dirtied herself with the blood and tears of the poor she nursed.

For this, she was loved by the people, but thought rather odd by the nobility. Many good stories survive about her kindness. Among them is one that doesn't quite ring true, and another that seems perfectly likely.

As the first story goes, Elizabeth's husband Ludwig has

forbidden her to give away any more food. But the cries of the hungry one winter distressed her so much that she begins sneaking food out of the castle in a hamper hidden under her cloak.

Ludwig catches her in the act, and challenges her to lift the cloak. She obeys, but where the food should be, there is nothing but beautiful roses. An embarrassed Ludwig is forced to let her pass.

Now certainly the God who parted the Red Sea could have sent some roses in winter to help a saint in a jam. But what makes the story suspect is that she would never have needed to hide things from Ludwig. He adored her.

He was only eleven himself when his four-year-old fiancée was brought to his father's castle to live. They grew up together. Their arranged marriage turned out to be both a passionate romance and a union of great friends.

A more likely tale is one told by an aged and dying crusader about the young princess he had known many years before.

Elizabeth could not go about her realm without being besieged by hopeful beggars. Zealous knights always made sure their princess was safe. This one observed his lady closely enough to notice how one day, when she was out of food, money and clothes to give away, one last beggar was still in need.

He claimed she took off her glove with its decorative jewels and gave it away. He further claimed that he found the beggar, bought the glove, and had it sewn onto his helmet. He insisted that through feudal wars and crusades against the Turk, it had brought him home safe so that he could now die in his own bed.

Maybe Elizabeth should have given the glove to poor Ludwig instead. He died from fever far from her arms on a crusade to the Holy Land when he was just 27.

After that, Elizabeth became even holier, or, maybe, just mad. Her in-laws, and Ludwig's heirs, didn't have to tolerate her eccentricities anymore, and refused to let her continue her work.

She took her children and left the castle to wander village streets, giving away everything she had until she too was essentially a beggar. She did make arrangements for each of her children to be well taken care of and raised as nobility, but personally she took vows of absolute poverty and lived out her remaining days in a hospital nursing the poor.

If she was mad, it was the madness of mystic joy. In imitating St. Francis' total renunciation of all earthly possessions, she gave up a kingdom for glorious visions of the Kingdom.

Mother sails up the Mississippi

On the first day I arrived at a previous parish, the teenage custodian informed me that what the church in that town really needed was a riding mower. Somehow, kerosene had been poured into the old mower's oil reserve by mistake. I bought him a K-Mart $99.00 special to push around.

Before long, he ran over a rock with it. The blade was twisted badly. "It must be time to get that riding mower, huh Father?" I took the blade off and laid it on the driveway. Parking my Buick station wagon over one edge of the blade, I flattened out the other edge with a sledge hammer.

Next, he managed to break the pull rope on the starter on a Saturday evening after the hardware store was closed. I had to take the 48" lace out of my high-top soccer cleats to wind around the pulley, but at least we were back in business again.

Finally, the mower's handle broke off. I bolted it back on with quarter-inch tempered steel, and, just to be sure he got the message, covered the handle grip with brushed buckskin and replaced the plastic wheels with solid chrome alloys off of a '57 Schwinn wagon. When I left for my next parish, years later, he was cussing and swearing under his breath as he pushed the mower around the four-acre lawn followed by his three kids.

Persistence doesn't always pay off.

It did for Rose Philippine Duchesne though. She was a young French woman who set out to be a Visitation Sister. But before she could profess her vows, the French Revolution broke out. Anti-clerical elements in the revolution eventually dissolved most convents in France, and Rose had to go home.

She taught and nursed, and visited the poor and imprisoned. When things settled down, she became a Sister of the Society of the Sacred Heart, and prepared for fourteen years to be a missionary. Finally a message from the Louisiana Territory came. That huge area, now part of the young United States, was in need of all kinds of staffing. Mother Rose Philippine led a group of four others to the New World.

They docked in New Orleans in 1818, just a stone's throw from where the Café du Monde serves its delicious *café au fait* and *beignets* — coffee laced with chicory and cream, and squares of dough deep-fried and powdered with sugar — a completely balanced breakfast.

After six weeks, the Sisters headed up the Mississippi on a steamboat to St. Louis where Rose encountered her first disappointment. The bishop who had sent for them went back on his promise that they would work among the "Indians." Instead, he had them begin schools up in Missouri for white children.

After an initial failure at St. Charles, Rose founded an orphanage and novitiate at Florissant, two convent schools at Grand Coteau, an academy and orphanage at St. Louis, and finally another convent back at St. Charles. Her persistent hard work laid the groundwork for an Order that would eventually number over 500 Sisters working in all areas of the Church and society.

But Rose persisted in her desire to work among Native Americans, or as she called them in typical, 19th-century European terminology, "the savages." After 22 years in the United

States, she finally got the go ahead to help at a mission among the Potawatomi in Kansas. But was she still able to do the work?

At the last minute, the frail, 71-year-old Sister, no longer the superior, was going to be left behind in tears when three others set out for the mission. A Jesuit priest accompanying the expedition insisted she come, however. He had become so convinced of her goodness over the years that he said, "Her very presence will draw down all manner of heavenly favors on the work." The trip revived her.

The Potawatomi admired the kindly Sister who visited the sick and helped young girls with knitting. They called her *Quah-kah-kanum-ad*, Woman-who-prays-always. She showed them the same kindness and love she had always exhibited to those she lived with, and she offered up her sufferings on their behalf as her health got worse.

After just a year, she was sent back to Missouri as she was expected to die soon. Again though she persisted in prayer, in practicing absolute poverty, in sewing vestments to be sent to the missions, and in begging money on their behalf. She was always critical of any kind of show in religious life, and insisted on simplicity among her Sisters and solidarity with the poor.

She lived on until 1852, dying on November 18th, still persisting in her dream of going west to the Rockies to help the missions there.

POPE GELASIUS

The emperor is within the Church, not over the Church

At the height of the power of Imperial Rome, its emperors sometimes called themselves divine. Or, if they didn't claim divinity, at least they claimed to be the high priest of the state religion, the *pontifex maximus*, or pontiff, the mediator between the gods and the Roman people.

Of course, after Christianity became established and the emperors themselves became Christians, certainly all this changed. Or so one would have thought.

Instead, the tendency persisted for a long time, especially in the East, for the Roman emperors to see themselves as the head of religion as well as the head of state.

One of the first to call the emperors to task on the issue was St. Ambrose, bishop of Milan. Emperor Valentinian wanted the bishop to loan a couple of his churches to Arian heretics so that his mother and her friends would have a place to "worship" their Christ whom they considered not truly divine anyway.

Ambrose refused the request. He could have politely said, "We can't. Our liability insurance won't cover it." But more conscious of his place in history, instead declared, "The emperor is within the Church, not over the Church."

Later, popes like Leo the Great would further spell out the meaning of Ambrose's dictum, until Pope Gelasius in 492 gave it its most complete explanation.

The problem then was Monophysitism, the belief that Jesus wasn't exactly human because his human nature had been absorbed into his divine one. The Council of Chalcedon had condemned the idea as erroneous. One report has it that a lone bishop held out for the notion that no one should be condemned for the heresy, however, if he could say Monophysite ten times in a row very fast. The report's veracity has been questioned by most scholars.

After the Council, the matter should have been settled. But emperors in Constantinople sometimes saw themselves as healing rifts in the empire and in the Church by compromising with the Monophysites, welcoming them into the Church, appointing them bishops and silencing their critics.

Pope Gelasius saw this as threatening doctrine and the independence of religious authority. So in letters, sermons and instructions to the emperor, he consistently laid out the position that popes would take for centuries thereafter.

Gelasius explained that there is the secular realm of authority and the religious realm of authority, that the emperor had his proper place to play in the former but should stay out of the latter.

The pope went further still. He felt, since religious authority was responsible to God for the salvation of all, including secular rulers, that conflicts of jurisdiction had to be decided in favor of the spiritual leadership.

The lines of demarcation remained hazy then and have vexed theologians and philosophers in many ages. Gelasius was certain of his position though. He saw bishops as autonomous in their proper sphere, and he saw the bishop of Rome as primary among them because he was the successor to Peter, first among the apostles.

Gelasius's feast is celebrated November 21st, the date of his death in 496.

Exiled priests with no styrofoam cups

I always patronize Burger King whenever I can because the company is so wonderfully generous. I went into my first Burger King about eight years ago, and ordered a small, black coffee to go. I paid the clerk who promptly put an empty Styrofoam cup on the counter. I looked down at the cup and then up at the clerk, and then back down at the cup.

A look of surprise came over the young man as he realized I had never bought coffee there before. "Oh," he said, "The coffee urns are over to your left. Just help yourself. And Burger King gives free refills."

"Fantastic!" I thought. "Free refills!" I took that cup with me everywhere — New York, London, Rome. But last year, when I started to use it at Burger King's location just off the town square in Prague, I noticed coffee spilling through a large crack in its side. It must have happened when that lady sat on my bag at the train station to ask me directions in Swedish. At least I think it was Swedish, because she was tall and blond and spoke just like that chef on the Muppets. I had to buy another cup.

Too bad Burger King wasn't around when the Jesuits were being thrown out of country after country. At least they could have had a cup of coffee to go.

By 1750, the Society of Jesus had almost 25,000 members

scattered around Europe and the New World, with pockets else-where on the globe too. They ran universities, seminaries, shrines, and over 270 foreign missions. But being the most pow-erful community in the Church meant they had made enemies along the way.

Strict Jansenists thought the Jesuits were too worldly. Many Enlightenment thinkers considered them too mired in old philosophies and approaches to the world. Nationalistic leaders of Church and State suspected the Jesuit universalist outlook and solid allegiance to the papacy. Bourbon rulers in several courts saw them as a hindrance to the consolidation of their power, and lots of folks just wanted to get their hands on Jesuit lands, schools and plantations.

The first blow fell in Portugal where the monarchy ar-rested leading Jesuits on trumped-up charges and exiled all the rest. In 1762, the high court of France decreed the Jesuits should be suppressed, and the king ordered them to leave the Society and become diocesan clergy, or to simply leave period. Even in their home nation of Spain, Jesuits were accused of disloyalty to the throne of Charles III and ousted in 1767.

About 6,000 were marched to the coasts to board ships for any Italian ports that would take them. One of these was Joseph Pignatelli, who, some say, saved the Jesuits from ex-tinction. When Joseph couldn't land in Italy, he went to Corsica where he used family funds to organize living arrangements for about five hundred priests and students.

When the French took Corsica, Joseph found a home for his wandering Jesuits first in Ferrara, then Bologna, then Parma. Even though the pope himself gave in to pressure and dissolved the Society in 1773, Pignatelli never gave up. Some-times he was a public Jesuit, sometimes a secret Jesuit.

Pignatelli preserved all he could of the history of the So-ciety and maneuvered among courts and cathedrals to get the suppression at least partly lifted wherever he could. The Jesuits had some friends and the Bourbons had many enemies. So the Society still functioned quite officially in some places and clandestinely in others.

Gradually, the pendulum began swinging Joseph's way. In 1798, the pope told Pignatelli he could start taking in novices once again, and in 1806, the Jesuits in Rome got two colleges back that had been taken from them. By then, Joseph was provincial of all Jesuits in Italy, and had gotten the Society officially restored in Naples.

Diplomatic, dogged, sharp-witted, Pignatelli brought the Jesuits through some very tough times. But they also remember him for his humility, his attitude of service in trying to keep diminishing communities together, and for exercising authority over them always in the form of a request, never a command.

He died in 1811, just three years before the Society was completely restored, and his feast is celebrated November 29th.

JAMES OF THE MARCHE

How much would he give me for my old watch?

Oxford University has made an attempt to issue an edition of the Bible free from what it calls gender bias and other forms of verbal discrimination. Thus a term like "kingdom" might be rendered "reign" instead.

Critics who have already complained about biases the translators overlooked or solved insufficiently remember one voicing concern about whether the verse "seated at God's right hand" discriminated against left-handed people. One solution was to change the phrase to "seated at God's mighty hand."

I thought this entirely ignored the geography of judgment day, and suggested a compromise whereby the verse would be translated as seated to God's port or starboard side. Jesus did, after all, seem to favor fishermen. I've checked several bookstores, but it appears the idea hasn't caught on yet.

One who would certainly vie to be on God's starboard side in Paradise would be the Franciscan priest, James of the Marche. He always saw himself as one of God's right-hand men.

He defended God's cause against those he saw as heretics or as threats to the Church, or simply as sinners in need of reform. He preached in Italy, Germany, Bohemia, Poland and Hungary in the 1400's.

Those who denied the leadership of the pope like the Fraticelli, or diminished the role of the Church in salvation, like the Hussites, felt his wrath as an inquisitor. But his real desire was to convince those in error, not to condemn them.

In sermons and discussion, debates and disputes, James stood for traditional Catholic beliefs, but also for strict Franciscan poverty and for the reform of material abuses in the Church.

He was also a pawnbroker on the side.

That is, he and other Franciscans encouraged the formation of "montes pietatis," non-profit organizations that would loan money to the poor in exchange for some object the needy would leave in their care.

The amount of the loan might be around two-thirds of the value of the poor person's possession, and if the object wasn't redeemed within a certain amount of time, it would be sold off.

In itself, the practice was nothing new. Similar efforts to help the poor in need of some emergency cash had been tried in several places, but without much success. The cost of running the operation often exhausted the start-up funds initially donated to the organization.

The new twist that James and others encouraged was to charge a little interest to cover overhead. It was a controversial move. The Church had always been at least uncomfortable about the idea of charging interest on a loan, and sometimes downright outraged.

But many Franciscans defended the concept since it was just a small amount and was meant to benefit the poor. For James, it provided still another issue to debate, discuss, argue over and support. His side won out when Leo X and the Lateran Council sided with the pawnbrokers to the poor.

James of the Marche, who got his name from the district of Italy where he was born, ended his long career in the service of the Church in Naples where he died November 28th,

1476 at the age of eighty. He had been sent there to preach reform.

I don't know what opinion James would have about gender neutral language in modern editions of the Bible. But I'm sure he has one, and is defending it vehemently at the starboard side of God.

Francis Xavier

Just who was this Cheryl?

Last week, a package arrived at the rectory with no name on it but addressed to St. Vincent's. I figured it must be for me because it said, "A Gift For You From Cheryl and Co." Then, on the side, "Gourmet Classics." Someone had sent me cookies, about three hundred of them, individually wrapped for freshness. But who was this Cheryl?

The cookies were good, but they didn't last very long — a few for breakfast, a couple for dessert after lunch and dinner, and maybe just one or two more before bedtime. A volunteer who helps in our kindergarten suggested she take some to the children, but I reminded her that too many sweets weren't good for people so young.

I was as possessive of those cookies as the villagers of Idocin were of their land rights. They were hard-headed Basques who insisted that their liege lord had violated custom by pasturing far too many cattle on their common ground, beasts that ate up all the good pasture so that the peasants actually had to buy fodder for their own small herds.

They took him to court, and, when they lost their suit, refused to pay their fines. In 1512, he rode into Idocin with sixty armed retainers to collect what was owed him. The peasants gave him a few chickens and stalled for time. When he died, they thought they had won.

But his widow, Doña Maria, was as stubborn as they were.

She sued them back, and sent her eldest son, Miguel, to threaten reprisals unless they paid up for past damages, and rendered him the proper rights due a feudal lord. When he arrived in the village with fifteen soldiers, the peasants appeared to give in. They gave him a banquet, mutton for his men, and oats for his horses. They even let him cut down one tree as proof of his rights over the local forest.

But they never paid up. Miguel was still dragging the peasants through the king's courts in 1530, when he insisted he just had to have the money owed him to keep his little brother in college.

The youngest son of Doña Maria was up in Paris, far away from his native Navarre and his family's ongoing fight with the peasants. He had come under the controversial influence of a new roommate who was fifteen years older than he, and who had a lot more experience of the world.

This new student had been in trouble at his previous university, and was making problems in Paris too. It seems that he was tempting younger classmates to skip their Sunday philosophical disputations to go instead to a Carthusian monastery to confess their sins, receive communion, and meditate on what the newcomer called his "Spiritual Exercises."

Miguel's little brother Francis was completely taken with the fervor of this Ignatius who had come into his life so unexpectedly just as he was nearing final exams. As a young boy, at the family castle of Xavier, Francis knelt before an old crucifix to meditate on the sufferings of Christ. Now he felt this same Christ calling him to follow an ex-soldier from Loyola on his quest to purify himself and to save others with the Gospel.

Francis and four friends joined Ignatius to form the core band that would eventually be known as the Jesuits. In 1542, Francis went as far as any of them in carrying Christ to the world when he landed in India. He preached and taught and baptized. He followed two approaches that would always characterize his missionary work — an appreciation for native customs and culture, and the education of an indigenous clergy.

In 1549, he took his message of salvation to Japan, and in 1552, he was headed toward China. Francis caught a fever though, and died on an offshore island on December 3rd while he was waiting for permission to enter a land mostly sealed to Europeans.

St. Francis Xavier is credited with converting about 30,000 people to Christianity. And these were not mass conversions either. He doggedly sought out individual converts with the same tenacity with which his family and their villagers pursued their rights against each other.

As I finished my reading on Francis the other night, I also finished the last of the cookies Cheryl had sent, still wondering who she was. When I turned to my stack of mail, I found my answer. I had laid aside a letter about "Foundation Sunday" from the Catholic Foundation of the Diocese of Columbus because I had already told them we would hold our Foundation Sunday at a later date due to a parish conflict.

The letter explained that the program for Foundation Sunday entailed showing a brief film about the Foundation after one of the Masses so that folks could learn about endowments, planned giving and the like. The plan also included refreshments — a pot of coffee provided by the parish, and gourmet cookies sent by the foundation through something called Cheryl and Company.

Now, of course, I have to get another box of cookies sent. That should present no problem. I'll merely have to explain how some misguided kindergarten volunteer went and gave away all of the Foundation's cookies by mistake.

DUNS SCOTUS

One way to describe the effects of original sin is to admit that we're all human: we make mistakes, we sometimes choose evil over good, we give in to sinful desires even when we know better.

The Church teaches that Mary was somehow preserved from this condition from the very moment she was conceived. December 8th celebrates the promulgation of this doctrine by Pope Pius IX in 1854.

Pius felt strongly enough about Mary's Immaculate Conception to declare that those who denied it "suffered shipwreck of the faith."

But if Mary never sinned, does that mean she wasn't human like the rest of us? Does it mean that she alone never needed to be saved? According to the new *Catechism of the Catholic Church*, she did indeed need to be redeemed.

But her redemption was accomplished before time began, at a moment when God chose her to be the Mother of the Redeemer. To us who are bound by time, it might seem like she was saved retroactively before she even existed. But God abides outside of time.

The choice of Mary as Jesus' mother, her redemption through the saving actions of her Son, her Immaculate Conception before her own birth, can all be simultaneous events to a timeless God.

At least John of Duns thought so.

He was born in 1265 in Scotland, in the small town of Duns. In an era before last names are common, he came to be known as John of Duns in Scotland or Duns Scotus.

He became a Franciscan priest in 1291, and served as a renowned teacher of philosophy and theology at Oxford, Paris and Cologne. Like Thomas Aquinas, he wanted to arrive at a grand synthesis of natural and revealed knowledge, but he didn't live long enough to accomplish that goal. He died when he was just 42.

Scotus felt that the merits of Christ's saving acts were certainly sufficient to save beforehand the one who would give him birth. He championed the doctrine of the Immaculate Conception 600 years before it became official.

But was redemption the real reason Jesus was born? Did the Father have to send the Son to earth in order that we might be saved? It seems Scotus said, "No."

He felt Jesus came to earth as one of us because God loves us. It was all free choice. It's like saying Easter follows Christmas. It doesn't cause it.

Maybe Scotus didn't want to base the Incarnation on human sinfulness partly because he emphasized human goodness so much. To Scotus, each individual person was a being of worth and dignity, freely created by a loving God who asked for love freely given in return.

Life was a journey of choices regarding that love, and Scotus was optimistic about our ability to choose reasonably and well because of the goodness God had endowed us with.

He taught that free choices to love or to do good are nothing less than imitations of divine grace and generosity and that the free choice to love God is the greatest imitation of divinity of all.

Scotus wasn't always appreciated in his own time, and misunderstanding of his work has plagued his memory ever since. He's never been canonized, but in an age that so often emphasized humanity's sinfulness and distance from God, his was a voice in behalf of human dignity and worth.

ADELAIDE

Saint Adelaide said no. So did Mrs. Ackerman

In the Middle Ages, many Christians pursued holiness by withdrawing from the world into lives of prayerful seclusion. Adelaide's enemies tried to make her do just that time and time again. But right to the end she remained a major player in the royal intrigues of her day.

First she helped to settle a war in 933. She was two at the time. Her father, the king of Burgundy, also wanted to be the king of northern Italy. Hugh of Provence opposed him until Adelaide's father agreed to betroth her to Hugh's son, Lothair.

After an engagement of fourteen years, the young people were married, and ruled in Italy together. Their happiness was short-lived, however.

Years ago, one of my brothers picked all the flowers out of a neighbor's back yard, went to her front door, rang the bell, and tried to get the neighbor, Mrs. Ackerman, to buy them.

Pursuing a policy almost as brazen, a certain noble named Berengarius tried to take control in Italy for himself after having Lothair poisoned by asking Adelaide to marry *his* son.

Just like Mrs. Ackerman, Adelaide said, "No." So Berengarius locked her away in a castle on Lake Garda and it looked like her years in the limelight might be over before she was even twenty.

But as the story goes, a lone priest soon came to her rescue. He's known only as Father Martin, and it's said that he dug a tunnel to set her free, hid her in a nearby woods, and fed her only on fish he caught in the lake.

When the Duke of Canossa got word of her whereabouts, he in turn rescued her from such a monotonous diet and brought her to his own castle.

There she met Otto I who happened to be in town trying to conquer Italy for himself and add it to his German kingdom. It was another good match. They married on Christmas day. When the pope crowned Otto "Holy Roman Emperor," Adelaide automatically became empress.

She was a very capable queen, a supportive wife, and a mother of three boys and two girls. The people loved her for her charity to the poor, the Church loved her for her generosity to monasteries and convents, and Otto just loved her.

Unfortunately, Adelaide was twenty years younger than Otto, and she became a widow again when she was forty-two.

Otto II seems to have wanted more independence from his mother. He and his wife Theophonia made life at court so uncomfortable that Adelaide moved out to live with her brother.

She was known though as a peacemaker, one who didn't hold grudges, and she was always open to reconciliation. So her son eventually apologized, and she returned to the palace until his death when her daughter-in-law again forced her to leave. But Adelaide had staying power. She outlived her son's wife too.

When Theophonia died, her son Otto III was just a child. Everybody with influence knew there was one person who could be completely trusted to watch over the young boy and his empire. Adelaide ruled until her death on December 16th, 999 at the age of sixty-eight. She was on a mission of reconciliation at the time, trying to bring peace to her native Burgundy.

DAGOBERT AND WILFRID

<table>
<tr><td>

The homeless bishop meets the king with no throne

</td><td>

Ohio Northern University recently began a new service for its students in Ada: free transportation to area churches on Sunday morning. At the end of our 11:00 A.M. liturgy last Sunday, I told Catholic students that it was now a little known fact that Ada is the smallest town in Ohio with a "Mass" transit system.

</td></tr>
</table>

Similarly, St. Dagobert II is a little known fact in the history of the Church. He's not even a saint everywhere, just in heaven and a couple of places around northern France.

But he's important for what he represents and for the persons he knew. Dagobert's father ruled as a Frankish king who died around 650, when his son was still quite young. This was a very dangerous thing for a royal father to do back then. Young Dagobert was ousted from the throne by a disloyal official, and had to go into exile across the sea to Ireland.

Perhaps it was all for the best. Dagobert got a good Christian education in Ireland, which was enjoying a cultural heyday due to the intellectual achievements of its great monasteries. He then traveled to England where he met and married a beautiful princess and fathered several children.

He also came to know a certain Wilfrid of York who kindly gave him hospitality. Wilfrid was a principal actor in the struggle to see what brand of Catholicism would dominate the north of England — Irish or Roman.

The dispute wasn't over doctrine, but Church organization and style. Anglo-Saxon invaders had decimated Christianity in most of England. When missionaries returned to once more bring the Good News, they came from two directions, up from Europe and over from Ireland.

The two groups differed in when they celebrated Easter. So the whole Church year with all its feasts was confused. They had different ways to administer Baptism and consecrate bishops, and looked in different directions for leadership, some to Rome, and some to the powerful Irish Abbot of Iona.

It was all eventually worked out, but in the meantime the disagreements had serious consequences. Dagobert's friend Wilfrid was named bishop of York, but wouldn't agree to be consecrated by local bishops who appeared to him too Irish.

Instead, he went over to the continent to get consecrated, and was quite surprised and upset when he returned to find someone else in his place. Over his long life, Wilfrid journeyed twice to Rome to gain the pope's support for his claim as the rightful bishop of York.

On one of these journeys, it was Dagobert's turn to give the homeless bishop hospitality. For the young man's foes had had a falling out back home and murdered one another. Dagobert had found himself restored to the throne because with enemies like that who needed friends?

He relished Wilfrid's friendship, though, and tried to get the older man to give up the whole English dispute and simply be bishop of one of Dagobert's cities instead.

The young king represented that branch of Frankish nobility in search of good Church leadership to convert their subjects deeper into Christianity and away from lingering traits of paganism. He founded monasteries, encouraged missionaries, and was popular as a real friend to his people.

Other Frankish nobles had different pursuits, however,

such as snatching each other's kingdoms. It was one of these who had Dagobert killed during a hunting expedition in the forests of Lorraine on December 23rd, 679.

Local people began venerating him as a saint, but he never made the official Roman list. His friend Wilfrid did though, and enjoys a feast day every October 12th.

This book was designed and published by St. Pauls/ Alba House, the publishing arm of the Society of St. Paul, an international religious congregation of priests and brothers dedicated to serving the Church through the communications media. For information regarding this and associated ministries of the Pauline Family of Congregations, write to the Vocation Director, Society of St. Paul, 7050 Pinehurst, Dearborn, Michigan 48126 or check our internet site, www.albahouse.org